IQ in Question

IQ in Question

The Truth about Intelligence

Michael J.A. Howe

SAGE Publications

London • Thousand Oaks • New Delhi

SAGE Publications Ltd
6 Bonhill Street
London EC2A 4PU

SAGE Publications Inc.
2455 Teller Road
Thousand Oaks, California 91320

SAGE Publications India Pvt Ltd
32 M-Block Market
Greater Kailash-I
New Delhi 110 048

British Library Cataloguing in Publication data

A catalogue record for this book is available from the
British Library

ISBN 0 7619 5577 1
ISBN 0 7619 5578 X (pbk)

Library of Congress catalog card number 97–067535

Typeset by Photoprint, Torquay, Devon
Printed in Great Britain by The Cromwell Press Ltd,
Broughton Gifford, Melksham, Wiltshire

Contents

Preface

Struggling with the writing of this book, I chanced to hear a radio programme commemorating the Battle of the Somme, which had started 80 years previously. An aged veteran was relating how his platoon had advanced from the trenches one summer morning in 1916 into a barrage of fire-power that had left most of his comrades dead or dying. He was not an educated man, and his vocabulary was limited, but no listener could have been unmoved by that old man's failing efforts to hold back his anguish as he recounted his ever-vivid memories of that terrible day.

It is easy to forget the debts we owe to ordinary individuals like that old soldier. We are encouraged to believe that people should be ranked and rated and classified, and that a particular indicator of a person's quality, the Intelligence Quotient (or IQ), forms a reliable indicator of the extent to which an individual is capable of those kinds of achievements for which people are valued. Because the knowledge and the experiences of that veteran would not have been ones that equip a person to do well at an IQ test, in all probability he would have been classified among the unintelligent, the failures, those who deserve our sympathy but not much more than that.

As many writers on intelligence have pointed out, people with low IQs do not thrive in the modern world. They tend to be poor, and unemployed or working in poorly paid unskilled jobs. Compared with better educated men and women with higher IQs, they are more likely to get into trouble with the law. They may be inadequate parents and their marriages are prone to break down. We are informed that they often become addicts, dependent upon alcohol, cigarettes, or other drugs. Their life-styles can be violent, dirty, and unhealthy. They are likely to drift into membership of a self-perpetuating underclass, made up of other unhappy, poor, and out-of-control men and women whose self-destructive violence and absence of order in their lives make them a threat to the majority and whose lack of skills keeps them in poverty, barring them from the rewards enjoyed by those who fill the jobs and meet the responsibilities that intelligent people value.

The belief that we are threatened by a growing underclass is far from novel, but in recent times it has been reinforced by claims that intellectual differences have a firm biological basis. We are told that only extended birth control or the infusion of good genes can prevent the perpetuation of low intelligence. Apparent justification for that depressing conclusion stems from the approach to human intelligence and its assessment that thousands of students encounter in psychology textbooks. The story they learn there – and it is one that is still being forcefully pressed on readers in the 1990s in a number of books about intelligence, including at least one influential bestseller – is that there exists in each person a quality of intelligence that provides the driving force enabling some individuals but not others to become capable of the mental skills needed in order to prosper in a modern society. Because this underlying quality of intelligence that people are supposed to possess to varying degrees is largely inherited and has a biological basis, it is largely unchangeable. So for those people whose IQs are low, and their children, the future is bleak.

That is the story about intelligence that everyone is told. It has the merits of being simple, clear, and easy to understand. For many people it is a way of regarding human abilities that conforms with common sense. It fits comfortably with the view that social inequalities are not the avoidable faults of injustice or bad government but an inevitable consequence of people being unequal in the extent to which they are inherently capable. Prosperous and successful individuals find it a soothingly acceptable account. If IQ testing encourages us to underestimate the value of people who get low scores, such as our veteran of the Somme battle, so much the worse for them.

However, as I demonstrate in this book, that story about human intelligence is largely untrue. As an account of why and how people differ in their capabilities it is more fiction than fact. But it is a story which, if believed, can do immense harm. It claims to answer some important questions, such as 'What makes people intelligent?' and 'Why are some individuals smarter than others?' Yet the answers it provides are not remotely adequate. There is a failure to even look for the real causes. Saying that someone is intelligent because he or she has intelligence comes no closer to providing a genuine explanation than insisting that the reason why certain men and women are successful is that they happen to possess success.

Intelligence is real enough, but it is only real in the sense that success and happiness are real. It is an outcome – and an important one – but it is not a cause. Contrary to what we are told, there are no genuine grounds for the common belief that intelligence is what makes people intelligent. Intelligence is the abstract noun that denotes the state of being intelligent, but it is not the explanation for it. Just as the concept of happiness does not explain why someone is happy and success is not the reason for a person being successful, intelligence is neither an underlying cause nor a driving force. The actual reasons why some people are more intelligent than others are numerous. They are also far more complicated than is implied by the viewpoint that sees a quality of intelligence as the explanation.

Past critics of IQ have concentrated on the abuses of intelligence testing, but the real problems go much deeper. The received wisdom on human intelligence rests on unsound assumptions, faulty reasoning, and inadequate evidence. Even the most confidently stated assertions about intelligence are often wrong, and the inferences that people have drawn from those assertions are unjustified. *IQ in Question: The Truth about Intelligence* challenges widely trumpeted views on a number of issues, including the claimed racial origins of IQ differences, the apparently restricted changeability of intelligence, the assumption that intelligence is measurable in the way that physical quantities are measurable, and the use of IQ scores to predict high individual achievements.

Among the people who have helped to make it possible for me to write this book I would especially like to thank Steve Ceci, who constantly reminds me of the fragility, fluidity, and fragmentariness of human capabilities, and Roy Nash, who made me aware of the serious flaws underlying mental testers' claims to have created genuine measures of psychological attributes. Thanks also to John Sloboda and Jane Davidson, my partners in a collaborative study of the progress of young musicians that has helped me to reach the somewhat sceptical conclusions concerning the possible role of innate talent that I relate in Chapter 8. I am also grateful to have had the opportunity to read the draft of a forthcoming book in which Ken Richardson exposes some of the errors that plague current thinking concerning genetic contributions to intelligence. Ziyad Marar, Lucy Robinson, and the editorial staff at Sage provided generous help and encouragement. Wendy Williams saved me from making one particularly embarrassing mistake; those that remain are entirely my own. Finally, my thanks to Sylvia for her love and support.

1

Introduction

Being intelligent matters; it makes a big difference to human lives. Sharp men and women thrive. Problems are solved by astute thinkers. Questions get answered by those who are clever. Smart people succeed at challenges at which duller individuals fail. Astute planners move ahead.

It is hardly surprising that psychologists take intelligence seriously, and have looked for ways to assess the degree to which different people possess it. In the past hundred years huge energies have gone into the development and application of intelligence tests. The increasing influence of the testing movement, and the acceptance of the IQ measure of intelligence (standing for 'Intelligence Quotient') as a familiar element of our mental landscape, have been seen as major successes of twentieth-century psychology. The very fact that people today have so little hesitation about ranking individuals as being more or less intelligent is a reflection of the way the spread of intelligence testing has affected our everyday thinking about people and their capabilities.

The growth of psychological testing has contributed to a state of affairs in which many people share a widely accepted viewpoint concerning the place of intelligence in our mental lives. According to that view, human intelligence is a measurable quality that is possessed by different people to varying degrees, and constrains each individual's mental capabilities; it is seen as an inherent capacity determining a person's potential to succeed at those tasks and problems that call upon cognitive powers.

That perspective on intelligence is widely shared. In the folk psychology of the twentieth century it has become the authorized explanation of the differing intellectual capabilities of human beings. It is not hard to see why. It is simple, straightforward, and easy to understand. It agrees with common sense, and the fact that common sense can be deeply misleading, as Einstein insisted when he defined it as a deposit of prejudice laid down in the mind before the age of 18, is not one that is universally appreciated. The commonsense view of intelligence has implications that many find comfortable, such as the idea that the varying prosperity and success of individuals is a natural consequence of inherent differences in their personal qualities, rather than a product of arbitrary or unfair social stratification.

Many in the western world subscribe to that account as unreservedly as African tribespeople agree that witches are the cause of famine and desease. However, we shall discover that, despite its attractiveness, there are strong grounds for arguing that such a view is misguided. I shall demonstrate in this book that the explanation it appears to provide for the fact that people differ in their intellectual capabilities is unconvincing and almost certainly false.

Unfortunately, the testing movement and the commonsense view of intelligence that it has allowed to flourish have influenced our thinking in some disturbing ways. People have been encouraged to believe that intelligence is fixed and unchangeable, an inherited product of the genes that is no more under our control than the colour of our eyes or the size of our feet. That is a worrying conclusion, especially when combined with the common belief that any person whose measured intelligence is low will be seriously handicapped, and incapable of many of the activities that make human lives fulfilling and productive. A consequence – it is claimed – is that millions of people are doomed to eke out their lives in an inferior underclass, with the chances of that fate being far greater for some racial and ethnic groups than others.

These dire predictions have been seriously promoted in a number of widely read accounts of human intelligence that have appeared in the 1990s. In each case the authors have bolstered their assertions with evidence that appears to be compelling. They present a thoroughly depressing picture of humanity, in which a large proportion of the population is seen to be held back by their own insurmountable limitations. If their accounts were found to be correct, the situation would indeed be bleak. Regrettably, too, the consequences would be almost as bad if those views were not actually true but were widely believed to be. That is because a consequence of following the kinds of social policies advocated by believers in the immutability of intelligence would be to produce a state of affairs that involved many young people being deprived to an even greater extent than they already are of opportunities that could help them to enlarge their capabilities and improve their lives. Thus according to Richard Herrnstein and Charles Murray, the authors of a best-selling book on intelligence, *The Bell Curve: Intelligence and Class Structure in American Life* (1994), there is little point spending money on educational opportunities for people with low IQs, because whatever you do their intelligence will not be appreciably raised.

So it is important to know the real facts. Does the hard evidence actually support the belief that intelligence is immutable? Are individuals' intellectual capacities permanently constrained by their racial origins? Is it true that someone's measured intelligence level is decided by that person's genes? Does a low score in an intelligence test really make a person incapable of solving difficult problems or making creative accomplishments?

In this book I provide hard factual evidence showing that none of these widely accepted assertions is actually true. I show that the depressing picture that many people have been encouraged to believe in by apparently authoritative writers on human intelligence is false. I also raise some basic questions about the nature of human intelligence, and examine findings that provide clues to the actual causes of differences between people in their intelligence test scores.

Can Intelligence be Measured?

Intelligence is a fascinating as well as important topic, and as a young student of psychology, looking for answers to all kinds of questions about people and their varying capabilities, I eagerly looked forward to the lectures on intelligence that formed part of my studies. But my enthusiasm was quickly extinguished. The first disappointment came right at the beginning, when I learned about the approved solution to the important problem of specifying what intelligence actually is. After being told how hard it was to reach agreement about a definition, we students were solemnly informed that the matter had been resolved by decreeing that intelligence is what intelligence tests measure.

That struck me as totally absurd. It seemed to me that unless you know precisely what you are measuring you can never be sure whether or not you really are measuring it. However, since the position I was questioning was the accepted viewpoint among respected experts, I assumed that my failure to see any sense in it was a reflection of my own naivety. I told myself that as I grew more knowledgeable I would come to see the wisdom in the approved viewpoint.

As it happens, my initial reaction was sound, although the view that intelligence is what intelligence tests measure continues to be proclaimed in textbooks, with the senior author of *The Bell Curve* insisting that the measurement of intelligence has been the greatest achievement of twentieth-century scientific psychology. The possibility of measuring something – whatever it is – depends absolutely on our being able to specify what it is that is being measured, and with intelligence that has never been satisfactorily achieved. Unless we know precisely what we are trying to measure there is simply no way to know whether or not we are succeeding.

Of course, science often concerns itself with influential qualities of the physical world that, in common with intelligence, cannot be directly observed or properly defined, and it may nevertheless be possible to assess the magnitude of their effects. But doing that falls short of actual measurement. It is sheer nonsense to insist that intelligence tests are measuring something at the same time as stating that what that thing actually is can only be specified by reference to the contents of the tests. And yet, amazingly enough, that is precisely what actually happens with intelligence measurement. The situation is not unlike one in which scientists attempted to measure people's height without having decided on exactly what is meant by height. That would only lead to ever-decreasing circles of confusion.

The term 'mental measurement' has become a familiar one, and perhaps for that reason many people wrongly think that what is involved in the putative measurement of people's psychological or mental traits is broadly similar to the measurement of physical quantities such as length and weight. Since physical measurement is a reasonably straightforward matter, the assumption is that the same kind of measurement is possible with psychological characteristics. But that is not true at all, as becomes apparent when we compare what is actually achieved when physical and psychological qualities are assessed.[1] In the case of a physical quality such as length, measurement starts with agreement on a definition that specifies what length is, and from then on everything is fairly straightforward, with little room for disagreement. In contrast, the 'measurement' of a psychological quality is a far more arbitrary matter.

By way of an illustration, imagine that somebody wishes to construct a measure of human vanity. Like intelligence, and unlike the concept of length, vanity has no clear agreed-upon definition that specifies how it should be measured or makes it possible to check that it is being assessed correctly. In the absence of these features there is no basis for deciding on how vanity should be measured. The would-be assessor of vanity has no alternative but to fall back on the device of putting together a few questions that appear to assess whether someone is vain or not. If it turns out that people's answers to the questions correspond to others' judgements of vanity, it is likely to be assumed that a 'vanity test' has been successfully constructed. The test-maker may believe that the test 'measures' the extent to which different individuals are vain.

In reality, however, what is being achieved by the test is a far cry from the kind of measurement that is possible with, say, length. It falls short of real measurement in a number of respects. One problem is that the selection of test questions is a largely subjective matter, because with a psychological quality such as vanity, unlike a physical one such as length, there does not exist the kind of precise definition that makes it possible to say whether or not the collection of test questions forms a valid measuring instrument. Consequently it would be possible for two psychologists to construct very different 'vanity tests' that each claimed to measure vanity but which failed to agree about which of the individuals taking the tests were most and least vain. Another shortcoming is that there is no non-arbitrary way of deciding to what extent differences in test scores indicate differences in the quality, vanity, that the tests are supposed to measure. With length, the measurement processes that we use make it possible to say that, for example, one line is twice as long as another. But with a vanity test, there would be no comparable way of specifying the extent to which people differ. It could not be said that someone whose test score was twice as high as another person was twice as vain, and there is not even any agreement on what it actually means for one person to be twice as vain as another.

The measurement of intelligence is bedevilled by the same problems that make it virtually impossible to measure vanity. It is of course possible to construct intelligence tests, and the tests can be useful in a number of ways for assessing human mental abilities, but it is wrong to assume that such tests have the capability of measuring an underlying quality of intelligence, if by 'measuring' we have in mind the same operations that are involved in the measurement of a physical quality such as length. A psychological test score is no more than an indication of how well someone has performed at a number of questions that have been chosen for largely practical reasons. Nothing is genuinely being measured.

Dimensions of Intelligence

My second disappointment had to do with the kinds of intelligence that had been investigated. I was looking forward to gaining insight into some of the wonderfully varied ways in which we humans utilize our mental powers. I had also anticipated learning something about the richness of human abilities, and discovering how people gain their differing capacities. I wanted to know how individuals' experiences help them to adapt themselves to the unique circumstances of their particular lives. But here too my hopes were soon dashed. I quickly discovered that those questions about intelligence which most engaged my curiosity had been largely ignored by the scholars of intelligence and intelligence testing whose contributions had to be studied. It turned out that instead of directing their attention to human intelligence in its fascinating and sometimes confusingly rich variety, the test-makers had confined themselves to a view of intelligence that compressed it to a single dimension. Rather than making a genuine effort to come to grips with the marvellous complexity of intelligence, they had decided to impose order on it, at whatever cost. From the narrow perspective of mental test construction, doing that makes a certain amount of sense. From any other point of view – especially one concerned with understanding or explaining intelligence, or discovering why and how people differ – it makes no sense at all.

I did not realize until later that the particular specializations of those psychologists who developed intelligence tests and introduced them into general use did not equip them at all well for answering the kinds of psychological questions that most people find interesting, such as 'How do you make people more intelligent?', 'How does intelligence develop?', 'What causes a child's intelligence to increase or decrease?', and 'Why do individuals differ in their capabilities?' Yet for almost a century, people have looked for wisdom concerning intelligence and its causes to the makers of mental tests, despite the fact that they often lacked either interest in or expert knowledge concerning those questions about the psychology of intelligence that are vital to a genuine understanding of it. The developers of mental tests have seemed happy to be seen as experts on intelligence in all its aspects. And notwithstanding their lack of the expertise and knowledge that could have made their viewpoints better informed, they have not shrunk from pontificating about the nature and origins of human variability.

Wrong as it is, the assumption that experts on mental testing, or 'psychometrics', should be seen as being authorities on the nature and causes of human intelligence is even now rarely challenged, although the truth of the matter is that believing that mental testing specialists will necessarily be authorities on human intelligence is not unlike assuming that driving instructors will have expertise at designing motor cars. In fact, as is very evident from some books on intelligence, an author whose psychological training has concentrated on mental testing may be entirely ignorant of how the burgeoning science of mental life has extended our understanding of human cognition and its development, and of the highly complex operations of the minds that generate intelligent actions and solve intellectual problems. The impoverished version of human intelligence spawned by the mental testing movement is certainly tidier and more manageable than the real thing. But because their exploration of intelligence has been restricted to one narrow variant of it, even those scholars whose role in the development of intelligence tests led to them being seen as leading lights on the psychology of human intelligence have had little to say about the really intriguing questions that ask how and why and when individual human beings gain, extend, and use their differing intellectual capacities.

There is a relationship of a kind between human intelligence in all its splendid richness and the version that has been studied during a century spent promoting intelligence testing and the use of IQ scores. We can illuminate the connection between the two by imagining a scenario in which someone proposes to develop a test to measure another valued human attribute, female beauty. It is quickly discovered that doing so is far from easy. One problem is that there are many different ways of being beautiful; another is that people have varying ideas about what is beautiful. In the face of these difficulties, a solution is devised which brushes them aside. This involves starting with one particular idea of female beauty, the one encapsulated in a Barbie doll, and rating people according to the extent to which their appearance approximates it. In other words, the more similar to Barbie, the more beautiful a woman is deemed to be.

That makes an ostensibly objective and reliable way of assessing someone's beauty, but it is not one that a wise person would take seriously. It has the crippling limitation of being based upon just one kind of beauty, ignoring all the ways of being beautiful except for the one that is encountered in a Barbie doll. A proposal to adopt the Barbie doll measure as *the* index of female beauty and attach importance to individuals' scores would strike most people as ridiculous.

The way in which human intelligence is assessed parallels the Barbie doll approach to measuring beauty alarmingly closely. What happens in intelligence testing is that a score that is allocated to a person following a somewhat arbitrary sampling of a person's mental performance is seen as forming *the* measure of that individual's intelligence. Great importance is attached to a person's score, and millions of human beings have found their lives dramatically affected by the contrasting consequences of getting a high test score or a low score. Sometimes the way has been opened to someone getting a skilled job, or an opportunity for access to education or training. At other times, low test scores have led to doors slamming in people's faces.

How did that situation arise? It is a long story with many threads, but two particular motives seem to have been important for the men (and they were almost all men) who were responsible for the present century's approach to intelligence and intelligence testing. The first was the understandable if misguided desire to keep things clear and simple. In common with beauty, human intelligence in all its forms is too messy and complex to be easily quantified. For anyone looking for a way to construct a test that would sample someone's mental capacities and perhaps assist in the making of practical predictions about his or her competence to master the skills needed for a responsible job, it is tempting to assess just a few capacities. Unfortunately, once it proves possible to assemble a test for assessing certain aspects of intelligence it is easy to forget that the test neglects other, equally important, dimensions of intellectual ability.

There was also a second and less innocent motive leading the early makers of intelligence tests to replace intelligence in all its variety with an impoverished conceptualization of it. That was the desire to rank people, placing them in order and replacing all that is unique about them with a single number. As Aldous Huxley made clear in his satirical novel *Brave New World*, which appeared in 1932, doing so is a tidy way to categorize humanity, with a strong appeal to those who are anxious to order and control. It can be attractive to people who wish to defend the interests of a privileged minority and maintain an unjust distribution of wealth and power. With the post-Darwinian fading of the traditional belief in the idea of a natural order imposed from above by a deity, intelligence testing has helped defenders of the status quo to fill that vacuum. In particular, confidently asserting that differences between people in their capacities are not only measurable but also innate and immutable has been a way of seeming to lend credence to the view that social inequities are justified. That belief, as John Stuart Mill remarked, has been a major hindrance to the rational treatment of social problems, and a stumbling block to human achievement. It still continues to be.

It is easy to forget that a test score is no more than a test score. We can find ourselves starting to think that the score does not just tell us about the person's output on the occasion when the test was administered, but also provides some deep insight into the nature of the person that he or she is. From that point it is tempting to begin believing that the score *is* the person, or at least a reflection of their inherent qualities. As those who run prisons and concentration camps have long known, it is easier to deal with simple numbers than with complex individuals.

Reaching Absurd Conclusions

There is no denying that the twentieth-century approach to human intelligence and its measurement has been influential, despite its deficiencies. Yet every so often that approach advertises its fallibility by arriving at conclusions that are patently crazy. In one criminal court case in London a man was charged with conducting fraudulent international financial transactions on behalf of a bogus merchant bank. Defending the man, psychologists argued that since his measured IQ was only 80, well below the average score of 100, his limited intelligence would have stopped him undertaking the transactions he was accused of. However, despite this advice, the overwhelming evidence against the man led to him being convicted. Notwithstanding his low test score, he had shown himself to be a person of considerable intelligence. He spoke four languages, regularly won large sums of money at card games in London clubs, and had succeeded in amassing a substantial amount of capital. When interrogated in court he answered questions fluently and displayed a sophisticated understanding of technical banking terms. His obvious intellectual powers clearly belied his low rating at the psychological tests that are supposed to measure a person's intelligence. Only someone with an unrealistic faith in the merits of psychological testing could possibly believe that this man's IQ test score provided a valid indication of his real abilities, in the face of all the evidence to the contrary.

Another incident, some years later, involved me more directly. The correspondence section of *The Psychologist*, a periodical of the British Psychological Society, published a letter by a young graduate complaining that in connection with a succession of job interviews she had been forced to spend many hours taking intelligence tests that formed part of the selection process. She reported that repeatedly having to do these tests caused her much stress and anxiety, and she questioned whether the amount of useful information that the potential employers learned from them really justified the time and peace of mind she was obliged to sacrifice. I responded to her query in another letter. I noted that while intelligence test scores can be moderately useful predictors of someone's suitability for employment, there was little evidence of any extra benefit to be gained from knowing people's IQ scores in the particular circumstances she described, which involved employers already having access to other information about educational achievements and examination performance.

I would not have been surprised to find myself contradicted by other correspondents who were better informed than me about the findings of studies investigating the effectiveness of IQ scores as predictors of suitability for jobs, but that did not happen. What did occur was that a number of letters appeared demanding to know how I dared to question the value of intelligence tests, and insisting that test scores were self-evidently valuable. One correspondent assured me that since he had been regularly giving tests for many years, as a practitioner he was far better placed to perceive their utility than an outsider like myself. Perhaps I should have anticipated that my letter might alarm people who make a living from the business of intelligence testing; it may have seemed to threaten their careers by challenging rarely questioned assumptions about the merits of testing. Tellingly, however, none of the responses which my letter elicited were accompanied by any factual evidence or rigorous arguments to support my attackers' assertions. It occurred to me that, perhaps as a consequence of intelligence tests being widely used, people have started to think that testing people's intelligence *must* be a useful thing to do, simply because it has become such a commonplace activity.

Criticisms of IQ Testing

For all its successes, the approach to intelligence that has stemmed from the development of intelligence tests and the IQ measure has never lacked critics. Some have called it a pseudo-science. Particularly damaging attacks were made by Stephen Jay Gould in his book *The Mismeasure of Man* (1984) which described an appalling record of questionable testing procedures, scientific wrongdoing, and other dubious practices. Gould documented the fact that on many occasions tests have been grossly misused, often in order to appear to legitimize unfair discrimination against minorities. He identified strong elements of racialism in some of the individuals who were active in promoting intelligence testing. Gould also demonstrated how abuses of testing have led to Jews, black people, and other groups being branded as feeble-minded. He also provided disturbing evidence of an unhealthy enthusiasm for eugenics among the pioneers of mental testing.

Not all the criticisms of intelligence testing have struck home. Some of the opponents have gone too far, asserting that the dominant approach to intelligence is largely based on pseudo-science. Undoubtedly there have been some bogus or fraudulent claims, such as those identified by Gould and the ones that came to light in connection with the research of Sir Cyril Burt. By and large, however, investigators have not been intentionally misleading. Numerous errors have been made, typically as a result of faulty inferences or reliance on inadequate evidence, but honest scientists do make mistakes. Eighteenth-century scientists were convinced that the air contained a substance called phlogiston. Even at the time of Einstein's twentieth-century discoveries, many physicists took for granted the existence of the ether, which was thought to be an invisible substance through which light and sound were transmitted. The fact that scientists can be massively in error does not automatically make them pseudo-scientists.

Some criticisms were easily refuted because they were directed at aspects of intelligence testing that are either justified or unimportant. For example, much was made of the objection that intelligence tests are unfair to certain minorities. There are various ways in which a test might conceivably be unfair to certain groups of people, but support for the charge of unfairness typically took the form of demonstrations that in order to do well at certain test items a person has to possess knowledge that is more likely to be familiar to middle-class testees than to individuals from other social and economic backgrounds. However, it turns out that whilst there is some justification to that criticism, it has been possible to defend intelligence testing against it by showing that the varying levels of test success associated with different social groups are not confined to just those tests for which the objection is valid.

But there is a similar criticism that is far harder to counter. This is that however much care is taken with selection of test items, mental testing inevitably favours those people who are most prepared to take on the challenge of being assessed. Individuals who are self-confident, competitive, and eager to display their abilities have a big advantage over those who find the experience of being tested threatening or irrelevant, or whose cultural values and expectations are not in accord with the view that it is desirable to exert oneself competitively when confronted with a test. People from minorities or social groups whose attitudes and social values are not compatible with enthusiasm for competing at mental tests often fail to do themselves justice.

Ironically, the sheer strength of negative feeling about intelligence testing and its likely dangers has sometimes had the effect of blunting legitimate criticism and debate of the issues. In the face of findings that seemed to have alarming social implications, there has been a tendency to politicize the debate on intelligence, or even to regard certain issues as being taboo. These reactions have impeded objective assessment. And critics have sometimes reached over-hasty conclusions. Humane scientists such as Arthur Jensen were vilified for arriving at controversial conclusions about intelligence. After evidence of malpractice had been identified in the data of one leading researcher, Cyril Burt, it was wrongly concluded by some writers that the case for a genetic contribution to intelligence had been demolished.

Many liberal-minded people have been unnecessarily alarmed by research results indicating that, first, there exist differences in the average scores obtained by people from different racial groups, and that, secondly, genetic factors contribute to a person's measured intelligence. These findings caused concern because they were thought to point to the existence of racial differences that are inherent and immutable. In reality, however, it can easily be shown that such a conclusion is not justified. In any case, most scientists would agree that any undesirable consequences that might conceivably follow from attention being drawn to ways in which racial groups are not identical are far outweighed by the negative social consequences of imposing a taboo on the issue. Doing that keeps everyone in a state of ignorance, allowing the wildest assertions to flourish unchecked.

Pressing Concerns

New and racially tinged variants of old controversies about human intelligence have surfaced in the 1990s. They add urgency to the need to highlight the mistakes and fallacies that bedevil psychological approaches to intelligence. *The Bell Curve*, by (the late) Richard Herrnstein and Charles Murray (1994), is just one of a number of books that have corralled data obtained from testing people's intelligence in order to promote right-wing social policies. That book caused particular concern because it promotes divisive policies with strong racial aspects, which these right-wing authors believe to be justified by evidence obtained from testing the intelligence of various categories of people. An even more overtly racial agenda is encountered in J. Philippe Rushton's *Race, Evolution, and Behavior* (1995). Rushton thinks that it is possible to identify racial groups that have clearly distinct and contrasting evolutionary histories, which have differently shaped the patterns of individuals' qualities and abilities. A third book on intelligence, entitled *The g Factor* (Brand, 1996), attracted the attention of the media in 1996 when it achieved the rare notoriety of being withdrawn by its British publishers, soon after its author, Christopher Brand, had announced that he was 'perfectly proud to be a racist in the scientific sense'.

These authors, among others, make numerous alarming assertions which in my view are wrong or misguided, and which if widely accepted have the potential to do major harm. I believe that it is important to expose those claims that are false and draw attention to the unreliable evidence, mistaken inferences, and faulty arguments that they depend upon. In writing the present book I have set out to do this. The book examines what is known about human intelligence in a manner that whilst acknowledging the genuine achievements of the past century does not neglect to draw attention to the many errors and abuses. It also shows how easy it is to neglect evidence that contradicts one's own point of view, and how the known facts can prompt invalid inferences and unsound conclusions which may have dire social consequences.

Testing can be an innocuous activity. Driving tests help us to decide when it is safe to allow people behind a steering wheel. A test in reading may aid a teacher's efforts to know how a child is progressing. An intelligence test, too, can be useful, providing information that can aid the making of predictions about an individual's future progress at school. But with intelligence testing, things have gone badly wrong, in ways that never happened with other tests, largely because all kinds of dubious claims have been made about the meanings and implications of a person's scores. The resulting state of affairs is not entirely unlike the situation that would arise if we started taking someone's performance in a driving test as being a permanent indication of his or her inherited capability to drive, dooming everyone who failed at the first attempt to a lifetime of dependence on public transport.

Note

1. An excellent discussion of the failure of psychometric tests to provide genuine measurement is provided by Roy Nash, in his book *Intelligence and Realism: A Materialist Critique of IQ* (1990).

2

Doubtful Beginnings

It began innocently enough, with a French psychologist named Alfred Binet. In 1904 Binet was asked to devise a diagnostic instrument for differentiating between schoolchildren of normal ability and pupils who were too far below the average to profit from the usual school curriculum, and therefore better suited to special schooling. Binet knew of the largely unsuccessful recent efforts of a number of individuals, including Charles Darwin's cousin Francis Galton, to construct tests that would assess individuals' mental capacities. He had already made some tentative attempts himself.

The test that Binet and his student Theodore Simon constructed was published in 1905. It contained 30 items requiring mental tasks of various kinds to be performed. These included easy ones that required children to do things such as attend to simple instructions, name parts of the body, compare lengths and weights, and remember sentences and lists of digits. There were also more difficult problems such as ones that involved indicating differences between objects and observing similarities, copying designs from memory, placing weights in order, providing rhyming words and filling in the missing words in sentences, making sentences that included words that were provided, and forming appropriate questions for various situations.

Because their construction has never been guided by any formal definition of what intelligence is, intelligence tests are strikingly different from genuine measuring instruments. Binet and Simon's choice of items to include as the problems that made up their test was based on purely practical considerations. The way in which some questions were devised and put together to form the test was not much more systematic than the method of constructing the 'vanity test' that was outlined in Chapter 1, or than the manner in which a journalist might act when told by his editor to put together some questions to form an 'Are you attractive to the opposite sex?' test. One can imagine the journalist cobbling together a list of items such as 'Do eyes light up when you enter a room?', and 'Have you ever been propositioned by . . . ?'. The test might even be validated up to a point, for instance by establishing that people with a substantial number of 'Yes' responses are more likely to have a sexual partner than those with a low score. But to claim that the test would be a 'measure' of anything would be clearly absurd: all it would consist of is a few questions that have been assembled together.

Intelligence tests are not totally different from that. In the case of the Binet and Simon test, since their main purpose was to help establish whether or not a child was capable of coping with the conventional school curriculum, they sensibly chose items that seemed to assess a child's capacity to succeed at the kinds of mental problems that are encountered in the classroom. Importantly, the content of the first intelligence test was decided by largely pragmatic considerations rather than being constrained by a formal definition of intelligence. That remains largely true of the tests that are used even now. As the early tests were revised and new assessment batteries constructed, the main benchmark for believing a newer test to be adequate was its degree of agreement with the older ones. Each new test was assumed to be a proper measure of intelligence if the distribution of people's scores at it matched the pattern of scores at a previous test, a line of reasoning that conveniently ignored the fact that the earlier 'measures' of intelligence that provided the basis for confirming the quality of the subsequent ones were never actually measures of anything. In reality, as we saw in the previous chapter, intelligence tests are very different from true measures (Nash, 1990). For instance, with a measure such as height it is clear that a particular quantity is the same irrespective of where it occurs. The 5 cm difference between 40 cm and 45 cm is the same as the 5 cm difference between 115 cm and 120 cm, but the same cannot be said about the differing scores gained in a psychological test.

As the years have passed, the techniques used in constructing and modifying intelligence tests have become increasingly elaborate and sophisticated. Nevertheless, it remains true that the tests currently in use are the descendants of batteries made up of questions that were assembled on the basis of largely practical considerations, rather than evolving from measuring instruments based on a definition of intelligence. If only for that reason, the idea that intelligence tests perform a measuring function that is comparable with the measurement of physical quantities is completely mistaken. As we shall see later in this chapter, a number of the misuses of data from intelligence tests have stemmed from the incorrect assumption that test scores do represent genuine measures.

Applying the Early Tests

The test originally devised by Binet and Simon appeared to be effective for its purpose, although the authors identified a number of weaknesses which they tried to eliminate in revised and extended versions that appeared in 1908 and 1911. The 1905 test was only suitable for young children. The 1911 test could be used by older children and also contained some items for adults. Binet's tests were said to measure the mental age of testees, enabling a child's intelligence in relation to others to be assessed by comparing the same individuals' mental and chronological ages. Different procedures were adopted with subsequent intelligence tests, in which a child's IQ score is based on a comparison between that individual's performance and the performance levels of other children of the same age. Alfred Binet died in 1911, but by then it was already clear that psychological tests could be useful instruments. Lewis Terman and others adapted and revised his materials in order to produce a test suitable for American needs, the Stanford–Binet, and other tests appeared later, such as David Weschler's Adult Intelligence Scale (WAIS) and his Intelligence Scale for Children (WISC). Especially in the United States, considerable energy went into developing and refining mental tests for children and adults, and by 1920 they had been adapted for adult personnel selection purposes as well as being applied in educational contexts. During World War I the necessity to select servicemen for a variety of different roles provided plenty of opportunities for the use of intelligence tests to be extended, and resources became available for developing new and improved psychological tests. At around this time the abbreviation

IQ (for Intelligence Quotient) came into use for designating a person's level of intelligence, and it continues to be widely used.

A cursory examination of the differing IQ scores obtained by a large number of people shows that they vary from 50 or less to above 150, with the average score being around 100 and the majority of individuals having scores that are not far from the average. Consequently, the distribution of people's scores takes the form of the familiar bell-shaped curve. The scores are said to be 'normally' distributed, and someone knowing the extent to which scores vary will be able to calculate the proportion of scores that are above or below a given value. It can be very useful to possess this information when one is interpreting test scores.

However, it is often wrongly assumed that the fact that IQ scores have a bell-shaped distribution implies that the differing intelligence levels of individuals are 'naturally' distributed in that way. This is incorrect: the bell-shaped distribution of IQ scores is an artificial product that results from test-makers initially *assuming* that intelligence is normally distributed, and then matching IQ scores to differing levels of test performance in a manner that results in a bell-shaped curve. This is a legitimate procedure provided that it is remembered that the bell-shaped distribution of scores is an artificial product rather a reflection of something that exists in nature.

Unsurprisingly, in the early days there were plenty of misuses of the unfamiliar new intelligence tests, and people's scores were often wrongly interpreted. For instance, it was often assumed that the typically low scores of would-be immigrants to the United States indicated inherent stupidity. There was a frequent failure to notice that a person's test performance could be sharply reduced as a consequence of unfamiliarity with the English language. More seriously, wanton abuses were also common. Racists and advocates of eugenic measures of social control were quick to seize on any tendency of the members of minority groups to do relatively poorly at intelligence tests. Low scores were regarded as providing evidence that legitimized discriminatory and oppressive social policies, as Stephen Jay Gould has amply documented in his book *The Mismeasure of Man* (1984). Leading psychologists such as Lewis Terman enthused about the spread of testing as an instrument of social control. Terman confidently predicted that testing would not only lead to 'curtailing the production of feeble-mindedness' but would also eliminate 'an enormous amount of crime, pauperism, and industrial inefficiency' (1916: 6–7).

Spearman and Intelligence Theory

As intelligence testing became a relatively commonplace activity and the tests themselves were increasingly refined it could have been expected that the abuses would diminish and that users of the tests would bring more sophistication and wisdom to the job of interpreting people's scores and making use of them to assist in the making of decisions. It certainly became possible to calculate the extent to which intelligence testing was effective for achieving particular aims. This can be done by assessing, for instance, the degree to which the introduction of test scores improves educational or vocational selection processes. It is possible to calculate the extent to which having a person's test scores available enables more accurate predictions to be made about that individual's future performance. So it might have been reasonable to anticipate that with tests that were becoming increasingly sophisticated and more widely accepted, the practice of mental testing would eventually come to be regarded as relatively uncontroversial, and no more than the application of a range of procedures designed to provide useful information about individuals' differing capabilities.

That did not happen, however, and intelligence testing has continued to be controversial, often encountering hostility and alarm rather than being welcomed as a useful psychological instrument. Why? One reason is that, from the outset, the practical application of mental tests was coupled with a theoretical viewpoint, sometimes labelled 'intelligence theory', that has been shared by most writers on intelligence, especially those whose claim to be authoritative is based on an expertise in 'psychometrics', or mental measurement.

Intelligence theory, which regards intelligence as a kind of faculty of the mind, is rooted in events that took place even before the publication of Binet's first test in 1905. Around the turn of the century, a young English army officer named Charles Spearman, who, like Binet, has been widely revered as a founding father of psychological testing, became interested in the possibility of applying to measures of performance at psychological tasks a newly developed technique for estimating the possible links or 'correlations' between sets of scores. Spearman quickly convinced himself that examination of the relationships between people's scores at different mental tasks would help to reveal some underlying quality of the mind that played a part in all mental abilities.

Spearman, a member of the Eugenics Society, had a clear agendum right from the outset. He knew that some scholars believed that a person's abilities were to a large extent the products of learning and experience. For instance, the great nineteenth-century thinker John Stuart Mill had argued that differences between individuals in their capabilities are largely the outcome of differences in their experiences. But for reasons that Spearman never made entirely clear, he thought that viewpoint not just wrong but positively immoral. Although Mill was in many respects the epitome of sobriety and seriousness, Spearman appeared to associate his ideas with a kind of hedonism that he abominated. For Spearman it was vital to believe that differences between people in their inherent qualities rather than in their experiences provided the explanation for their varying capabilities.

We cannot be certain why Spearman took that stance, but it is possible that he, in common with many anxious spectators of the Darwinian revolution, saw challenges to his own viewpoint as threatening the established order which dictated that each individual should remain in his or her allotted position within the social hierarchy. In any case, Spearman's apparent inability to separate his views about what was morally desirable from his thoughts concerning the causes of people's abilities was an unfortunate lapse in someone who was to become a pivotal figure in the development of a modern approach to human intelligence. Scientists do need to be open-minded: thinking that is straitjacketed by dogmatic beliefs can lead to pseudoscience rather than genuine scientific progress.

Spearman regarded a person's intelligence test score as being far more than an indication of a person's mental output, or a mere measure of someone's capability to perform mental tasks. He saw intelligence in a very different light. For him it was not just a product, but a kind of power source for the person's capabilities. For Spearman and his successors intelligence was the underlying cause of a person's performing at whatever level he or she attained, with differences between people in their intelligence being the fundamental reason for their differing success at mental problems.

Whether or not Spearman was justified in believing that intelligence tests are not simply a way of assessing people's mental abilities but also a way of accounting for them continues to be a matter of dispute. An objection is that making such an assumption is rather like believing that by devising a test that makes it possible to assess and compare the productivity of different factories one is also explaining *why* some factories are more productive than others, or akin to believing that an indication of someone's success in life explains why the person is successful. Certainly, however, Spearman was by no means alone in taking the view he adopted. For those who share it, intelligence is what makes a person intelligent: it is an underlying quality that enables a person to succeed at mental tasks and solve problems, including those that are encountered in intelligence tests.

Intelligence as a Mental Faculty

Considered in this way, intelligence is a kind of faculty of the mind: it is the mental faculty that makes a person intelligent. What is meant by a faculty of the mind? That concept arises from a way of perceiving the brain as being divided into various parts that directly correspond to its observable attributes and capabilities. For instance, a believer in faculty psychology may assume that because people exhibit qualities such as self-esteem, cautiousness, attentiveness, spirituality, honesty, hope, combativeness, and' so on, they must possess corresponding underlying mental faculties of self-esteem, cautiousness, et cetera. Thus in order to account for the observation that an individual is, say, unusually spiritual, it is postulated that the person has an especially powerful faculty of spirituality.

That once popular but now outmoded approach has its attractions, but it also has limitations. In particular, it tends to encourage faulty inferences about the underlying causes of observed events and qualities. That is readily demonstrated by looking at the results of applying the same kind of reasoning in attempts to explain various other kinds of happenings. Imagine, by way of illustration, that a person who has spent her life on a small rural island visits a manufacturing region for the very first time. She is taken around a couple of factories and is told that one is more productive than the other. Being of an inquiring frame of mind she carefully examines them – a sensible thing to do – but her examination takes the unhelpful form of an attempt to identify the part of each factory wherein the productivity resides.

We can see that such an approach to the problem is bizarrely mistaken, although the woman's reasons for taking that approach are not totally illogical. She has assumed, wrongly but quite understandably, that if the two factories exhibit productivity, the causes of it must lie in some kind of productivity mechanism (or faculty), and that the reason for the factories' differing productivity is that one has a stronger or better developed productivity mechanism than the other.

Alternatively, imagine that a man with no mechanical knowledge is given a new car. He is curious to find out how it works, and learns that it possesses a number of attributes, including power, speed, and smoothness of running. His investigative strategy is to conduct a careful examination of the parts, looking at each of them and trying to decide which is responsible for the speed, which determines the power, and which part creates the car's smoothness.

In both these cases we can see that the individuals' efforts are misdirected. Each person has gone astray largely as a result of wrongly assuming that there must be a close correspondence between the terms that *describe* performance or output, in terms of its various attributes, and the actual causal mechanisms that *explain* or account for that performance. At least two kinds of faulty thinking are evident here. First, there is the presumption that the manner in which we choose to label the various observed functions of a car (or factory, or human brain) tells us about the nature and organization of the underlying processes and mechanisms. Secondly, it is believed that a concept that has been introduced to describe what is achieved (productivity or speed, for instance) can also help explain the workings that give rise to that performance. This kind of thinking is evident when someone believes that because the car is seen to exhibit speed, there must be an underlying speed component, or that if a factory has high productivity, the cause must reside in a productivity faculty. Similar reasoning may lead a faculty psychologist to deduce that because somebody is a determined man he must possess a strong faculty of determination or will.

Phrenology

The trouble with faculty psychology is that when following that approach in order to try to explain psychological phenomena it is difficult to avoid making logical errors like those above, as was already evident by the time the first intelligence tests were constructed. However, in the early part of the nineteenth century faculty psychology had received a powerful boost from an approach known as 'phrenology': this appeared to demonstrate that faculty psychology had some physical basis in the structure of the brain. Phrenologists believed that signs of mental faculties could be located on various parts of the skull. Thus a bump on one part of the head would be seen as evidence that a person possessed an enriched faculty of spirituality, and a depression elsewhere on the skull might be thought to denote diminished self-esteem or impaired honesty.

Yet it soon became obvious that the phrenologists were in error. They were correct in observing that many functions of the brain are localized and operate in a relatively autonomous or 'modular' manner, but the way in which the human brain really works is far more complex than they appreciated. Phrenology, in common with faculty psychology, is flawed because it relies upon the same faulty reasoning processes that mislead a person into thinking that there is one part of a factory in which its productivity resides, or a particular component of a car in which its speed can be located. In reality, the brain is much more than a conglomeration of separate mechanisms that correspond in any straightforward manner to its observed psychological outputs. The operations of the human brain are made possible by the joint activity of a large number of extremely complicated mental computing systems. As in most complex systems, there are numerous ways in which output levels can be influenced. Just as there are many elements of an engine that can affect its speed, there are numerous different ways in which the human brain's output of intelligent behaviour can be affected. The belief that there exists some single cause or mechanism that determines how intelligent a person becomes is hard to reconcile with a proper awareness of the true complexity of mental functioning in the human species.

A General Factor: Spearman's *g*

Charles Spearman and his successors were not entirely unaware of the limitations of a faculty approach, but they nevertheless regarded intelligence as being something real, an underlying quality of the mind. For those who share this viewpoint, intelligence is not merely a descriptive term: it is regarded as an explanatory concept that explains why some people are more intelligent than others. Spearman believed that he had succeeded in identifying an embodiment of intelligence which demonstrated its reality as an underlying mental faculty. He reached this conclusion after applying a series of procedures which involved calculating correlations between people's scores on a variety of tests of mental ability, and then looking at the patterning of the correlations, using a technique known as 'factor analysis'. He was able to show that, algebraically, it was possible to demonstrate that much of the variability in people's scores could be ascribed to a single common, or 'general' factor.

Spearman became convinced that the emergence of a general factor provided evidence of some common underlying quality, in the form of a kind of mental energy, that underlies variability in scores at intelligence tests. For him, the finding that it was possible to demonstrate a common thread in the patterning of individuals' test scores was sufficient grounds to confirm his belief that there was a common influence underlying those scores. The indication of commonality, the general factor, could be expressed as a number, which Spearman designated by the letter *g*.

Spearman had indisputably arrived at an economical way of accounting for large arrays of different scores in terms of a small number of factors, in a manner that is not totally unlike a much more complicated version of the feat of accounting for numerous points on a line with one simple equation, such as $y = 4x^3 + 5$. But for Spearman, g was much more than a way of accounting for intelligence test scores in the sense of providing an economical way of describing them. For him it was a way of explaining them. The fact that the value of g was usually found to be above zero was seen by Spearman as proving the existence of an underlying mental faculty of intelligence, and he regarded an individual's g as an indication of that person's inherent intellectual level.

Thus g was hugely important for Spearman; he even favoured restricting the vote to individuals whose g index exceeded a certain level. In accordance with his enthusiasm for eugenics he went so far as to argue that only those individuals who were sufficiently high in g should be allowed to have offspring (see Fancher, 1985: 95). He was convinced that g was a kind of brain power or mental energy, and he believed that it was the presence of g that made a person intelligent. In short, Spearman thought that by deriving the g factor he had done far more than arriving at a good way of describing data relating to intelligence. He believed that he had discovered the actual cause of high intelligence. One person was highly intelligent because that individual was well endowed with g. Another person was less intelligent because he or she was low in g. That view was widely accepted by users of intelligence tests, and it still continues to be. As we shall see, even now, textbook writers and others promote the view that g plays a major role in making people intelligent.

But in reaching the conclusions he arrived at Spearman was making a mental leap of very dubious legitimacy. He was assuming that his genuine achievement in discovering, through the use of factor analysis, an economical way of *describing* variations in performance at the tasks comprising a mental test also gave him a way of identifying the mental mechanisms that cause or *explain* variations between people in their level of performance. In reality, however, factor analysis simply cannot do that. By demonstrating that a body of data can be shown to be structured in one or other way, factor analysis can certainly provide useful hints about possible underlying causes. However, because the data that are entered into factor analysis are exclusively data concerning products or outcomes, there is no way in which the algebraic operations that are undertaken in conducting a factor analysis, however complex they are, can succeed in identifying the mechanisms or causes that produce those outcomes. To assume otherwise is like thinking that if someone keeps observing how an aeroplane operates under varying conditions he or she will eventually discover exactly how it works, or that observing the performance of an automobile will lead a person to understand the workings of the internal combustion engine.

Even in its role of depicting structure in performance data, there are firm limits to what factor analysis can achieve. In particular, whereas it can demonstrate that this or that kind of structure can be perceived in a body of data, it does not identify any one unique correct solution. An everyday experience illustrates the reason for this limitation. If I examine the pattern on the wallpaper in my kitchen, I can decide that it consists of vertical lines of dots with various lines going in other directions, or alternatively I can say that the pattern takes the form of horizontal lines of dots with other dots positioned horizontally to those lines. Or I might equally legitimately decide that the dots on my wallpaper form diagonal lines, with other dots being positioned at right angles to those lines. The point is that there is no one uniquely correct description of my wallpaper, each of the above descriptions being equally valid.

Similarly with factor analysis. It allows one to verify that data can be said to be patterned in a certain manner. But there may be a number of alternative patterns to be discerned, and factor analysis does not identify any one pattern that is uniquely present in the data. And it certainly cannot identify any underlying structure that produces an observed arrangement or patterning of scores. In fact, factor analysis does not actually 'find' any pattern at all: it simply verifies or disconfirms the existence of a pattern of correlated scores that an investigator believes may be present. In essence, the investigator makes use of factor analysis to check the legitimacy of assuming that some data can be said to fall into such or such a pattern. Questions about *why* correlated scores are patterned or structured in a particular manner are an entirely different matter, and one that the techniques of factor analysis cannot decide upon.

The Meaning of Spearman's *g*

Perhaps surprisingly, Spearman persisted in his belief that in isolating the *g* factor he had identified the cause of differences between people in their intelligence. Even more surprisingly, a substantial number of contemporary writers on intelligence continue to hold this view, being 'unanimous in insisting that *g* sits at the centre of the structure in a dominating position – not just as an artifact of statistical manipulation but as an expression of a core human mental ability much like the ability Spearman thought he had identified at the turn of the century' (Herrnstein and Murray, 1994: 14).

There have been lengthy debates concerning whether the figures that emerge from intercorrelating intelligence test scores point to a pattern in which a primary element is a single general factor, or whether the same figures are best described in terms of a number of different factors. The statistician Godfrey Thomson pointed out in the 1920s that alternative ways of depicting the patterns of correlations were equally valid. Others have established that the finding that it is possible to extract a general factor when the appropriate analyses are performed on scores from a variety of mental tests may be simply a consequence of the fact that among the many influences that affect performance at each of a pair of mental tests, there are some that are common to both of them. These common influences may stem from similarities either in the tasks or in the underlying skills needed to perform them, or they may reflect the contribution of relatively stable attributes of a person that have similar effects on level of performance at each task, such as attentiveness, persistence or self-confidence, or more fleeting influences such as level of fatigue or boredom.

However, the successors of Spearman have continued to insist that the *g* factor represents something real. They continue to regard it as a kind of mental energy that varies in amount or quality from one person to another and explains why people differ in intelligence. Thus in Christopher Brand's 1996 book *The g Factor: General Intelligence and its Implications*, the author insists that *g* provides the only way of predicting success in most occupations (1996: 32) and that high *g* conveys advantages valued by employers. He makes the demonstrably false claim that 'theorizing and research are rarely even attempted by those who are determined to doubt the reality of *g*' (1996: 50). He asserts that tests have repeatedly shown the meaningfulness of *g*, which he sees as having numerous important functions. Paul Kline, in *Intelligence: The Psychometric View* (1991), regards the measuring ability measured by *g* as 'a basic human characteristic' (1991: 145), citing an anecdote by Bertrand Russell about his childhood interest in Euclid as 'a perfect illustration of high *g* in action' (1991: 146). The authors of *The Bell Curve* are convinced that all tests of academic achievement measure the general factor to some degree and that IQ tests expressly designed for that purpose measure it most accurately (Herrnstein and Murray, 1994: 22). They also imply that *g* has a biological basis and is underpinned by neurological processes, (for example, 1994: 15, 284) and they state that black populations generally do better on test items that are less saturated with *g* and relatively worse on items more saturated with *g* (1994: 636). Similarly, J. Philippe Rushton, in *Race, Evolution, and Behavior*, is convinced that the *g* factor is the 'active ingredient' in human intelligence (1995: 34), that there exists 'convincing proof for the pervasiveness of *g*' (1995: 34), and that differences between races in *g* reflect genetic influences rather than socioeconomic ones (1995: 195).

In my view, however, there are no convincing reasons at all for insisting that *g* is something real, with a biological basis, as these authorities have continued to assert. This belief that there is a simple cause of differences between people in their intelligence is based upon a way of thinking about the manner in which the human brain does its work that was already outmoded at the end of the nineteenth century. Yet believers in the reality of *g* have claimed that the case for it is supported by evidence from research studies. These have looked for relationships between performance at intelligence tests and levels of success at very simple and basic mental tasks. A key argument here is that if it can be shown that intelligence test performance levels are closely related to indicators of fundamental processes of the brain, then an intelligence test score can be seen as an indication of something that is genuinely real, in the sense of being a fundamental cause of variability in intellectual abilities.

Brain Processes and Intelligence

It is conceivable that there do exist certain fundamental brain processes that inherently differ from one person to another in important characteristics such as the speed at which information can be transmitted. It is also possible that such variations could be a cause of differences between people in their intelligence. And if that scenario turned out to be a realistic one, it would appear to be true that intelligence test scores are influenced by processes that are basic to human cognition and also account for differences between people in the speed or efficiency of their mental operations. But to provide supporting evidence for that account, it would first be necessary to show that people do inherently differ in the speed or efficiency with which certain brain measures transmit information, and then provide evidence that intelligence scores are highly correlated with measures of this underlying brain speed or efficiency.

Some researchers have claimed that the necessary confirmation has been achieved. They base this claim on the fact that performance at some of the tasks included in intelligence tests has been found to be correlated to a modest extent with performance at very simple tasks that are believed either to reflect the operation of fundamental mental processes, or to provide relatively direct measures of the brain's physiological functioning, as is the case with the 'evoked potential' measures obtained with EEG instruments. When the research is conducted on groups of participants whose distributions of abilities match those of the population in general, the correlations are found to be relatively low, typically around +.3 to +.4 or less, which means that they 'account for' up to about 15 per cent of the variability in people's scores. (The latter is calculated by squaring the correlation.) All the same, the fact that there are positive correlations, however small, is consistent with the possibility that there do exist fundamental systematic differences between people in the functioning of their brains, and that the existence of such differences contributes to the fact that people differ in intelligence (see Howe, 1990: 197–223). The existence of correlations between scores is also consistent with the possibility that g is to some extent an indicator of the existence of such fundamental differences.

However, there are serious problems with this line of reasoning. A major one is that the belief that researchers have succeeded in identifying tasks that are sufficiently simple to justify the assumption that differences between people in performance at them reflects differences in the functioning of fundamental brain processes is probably wrong. Consider the actual kinds of tasks that have been selected. One, for instance, takes the form of 'reaction time' problems, in which a person's time to respond to a simple stimulus is measured. Another kind of task is known as an 'inspection time' problem. It involves a simple judgement, such as deciding which is the longer of two lines, the measure of performance being the time taken to decide. With tasks like these, it has been assumed that since performing them is a relatively simple matter and does not obviously depend to any great extent upon training, individual differences in people's speed at doing them provide evidence of innate differences between people, uncontaminated by differences between individuals in previous learning or in their experiences.

That assumption has been questioned, however, because it has become evident that a person's performance at even very simple mental tasks may be affected by learning and experience. In the particular case of observed correlations between intelligence test task scores and measures that directly reflect physiological functioning, there is the further problem that the existence of such correlations does not necessarily indicate that whatever processes underly differences in the physical measures play a part in actually causing differences in test scores. It is entirely conceivable, for instance, that differences in physical functioning are the result rather than the cause of differences in test performance. In short, whilst the observed correlations are consistent with the possibility that fundamental differences between people in mental functioning make a modest contribution to their differences in intelligence, there exists no strong evidence that such an account is correct (Howe, 1990a: 215). Moreover, by no means all research of this kind has yielded even modest correlations. In some instances the value of the correlation has been zero, indicating the absence of any relationship. Zero correlations are especially common in circumstances where care has been taken to choose simple tasks that are genuine components of the broader abilities assessed in intelligence tests, and thereby ensure that the simple tasks actually are based on qualities that are in a real sense fundamental ones (Keating et al., 1985).

A common misconception is that if there is evidence of physical differences in the structure of the brain that correspond to differences in intelligence, this demonstrates the existence of inherent differences between people in their intelligence. In reality, however, just as a person's intelligence can be affected by experience and learning, so too can the physical characteristics of the brain. Experience can produce changes in various parts of the brain. For example, in violinists and other string players the representation in the cortex of those digits that are involved in fingering the strings is larger than in other people, with the size of the difference being related to the age at which instruction began (Schlaug et al., 1995).

The Use of Adjusted Scores

The case for the view that the correlational evidence demonstrates that differences in intelligence depend upon fundamental differences in mental processing is further weakened by the fact even the modest correlations that have been reported are often not the ones actually obtained. In many cases they have been artificially inflated by a process of 'adjustment' that is almost certainly not legitimate. In reporting their findings, researchers have adjusted upwards the correlations emerging from their research, having convinced themselves that there is a valid reason for doing so.

Here is their reason for believing this curious practice to be justified. Imagine that you are attempting to calculate the correlation between the heights and weights of a group of people, but your measuring instruments are somewhat crude and unreliable, resulting in somewhat inaccurate measures. Because of this, when a correlation is calculated, based on these (inaccurate) measures, the obtained correlation is smaller than the real correlation, that is to say, the correlation that would have been obtained had the measures of height and weight been highly accurate ones. Knowing this, it would be possible to argue that when the magnitude of a correlation that has been calculated is known to be depressed by the inadequacy of the

measuring instruments, it is permissible to adjust the correlation upwards in order to provide a better indication of what the
correlation would have been if better measuring instruments
had been available.

Some researchers have introduced similar arguments in
respect to correlations calculated on mental tests. That is, they
have assumed that their measuring instruments have been
inaccurate and unreliable and that they are therefore justified
in adjusting their observed correlations upwards to provide a
better indication of the 'real' magnitude of relationships. However, it is quite wrong to do this, and the reasons why are
obvious when we compare the activity of measuring a physical
quantity such as weight or height with the activity of 'measuring' a psychological trait. In the latter case, unlike the former,
genuine measurement is not possible, for reasons that were
discussed in Chapter 1. To summarize the argument, in order to
engage in genuine measurement it is essential to define precisely what is being measured and how it is to be measured, and
it is also necessary to be able to know to what extent accurate
measurement is being achieved. With psychological traits such
as intelligence this simply cannot be done. It is not possible to
'measure' intelligence in the way that physical dimensions are
measured. So it makes no sense to say that one obtained score
provides a better or a worse measure of intelligence than
another, if only because there is no agreed criterion that provides a basis for making a comparison. Therefore, there can be
no justification for the practice of adjusting correlations upwards to reflect one's belief that the (so-called) measures that
enter into the correlations are inaccurate.

A final point. It is sometimes believed that if a number of
scores are correlated and the correlations themselves correlate
with one another, such a pattern of intercorrelations provides
evidence that there must be 'something in common' to all the
scores. In particular, the fact that it proves possible to extract
factors such as *g* is also thought to show that there is one
common influence affecting each of a large number of mental
test scores. This reasoning is fallacious, however, and that
becomes apparent when we direct our attention to the raw
scores that are correlated at the outset of the operations that
are conducted prior to a factor analysis. Correlational techniques start with comparisons being made between two scores

at a time. When something that affects one of a pair of scores also affects the other score, the chances are that a positive correlation will be found when a number of such pairs are examined. However, the reverse does not necessarily apply. That is, one cannot assume that whatever underlies the similarity between one pair of scores is the same as the influence that contributes to the similarity of another set of scores. The influences that have led to some pairs of scores being alike may be entirely different from the influences that have led to similarities in other sets of scores. Within the procedures involved in factor analysis there is simply no way of knowing about that.

There are numerous possible reasons for any two sets of scores being correlated, and there is rarely any firm justification for believing that such a correlation shows that both sets of scores must be affected by some quality that is directly related to intelligence. Many of the numerous possible influences that can lead to two sets of IQ scores being related are unrelated to intelligence as such. Imagine, for example, some of the circumstances that could lead to a person performing relatively well at each of two different tests, or relatively poorly at both of them. In the first place, it is frequently the case that apparently dissimilar tasks share elements in common. The different tasks could draw upon the same body of knowledge, or they could both involve the same mental skill. In either case, the result would be positively correlated scores.

In addition, there are a large number of personal traits that might exert similar effects upon a person's level of performance at two different test items, and thus lead to scores being related to one another. Examples are an individual's competitiveness, enthusiasm to do well, attentiveness, ability to concentrate, test-wiseness, patience, self-confidence and doggedness. Also, the effects of even transitory influences such as fatigue or boredom may not be restricted to one particular item, and performance at a number of tasks could be similarly affected. Any of the above influences, and any combination of them, may contribute to a state of affairs in which scores at different tasks are related, so that not only would sets of scores be correlated, but the application of factor analytic techniques to data obtained from administering intelligence tests to a number of people would result in certain factors or components being identified. Many collections of scores, when submitted to the kind of analyses performed by Spearman and his successors, will reveal a common factor, but the fact that this happens does not mean that one common cause has been identified.

Conclusion: Does Intelligence Actually Exist?

This chapter began by sketching the early development of intelligence tests. A number of limitations were identified. A person's IQ score, which is based on his or her performance at an intelligence test, gives an indication of mental output. However, beginning with Charles Spearman, intelligence theorists have argued that test scores are more than mere indicators of output, and reflect some underlying quality that makes people intelligent. According to Spearman, the general factor, *g*, points to such a quality, which provides a source of mental energy. That view is still widely accepted and influential, but the arguments for it are unconvincing.

Does intelligence exist? In two different senses of the word, the existence of intelligence has never been in doubt:

(1) As a general umbrella term referring to a range of questions and issues that relate to human intellectual abilities, the word 'intelligence' is a useful and necessary one for largely the same reasons that other umbrella terms like 'economics' and 'gardening' are. Used in this way the word simply designates a broad field of interest. Someone who is concerned about why one person is more intelligent than another, or about how, why, when, and if individuals become more or less intelligent, can be said to be interested in the topic of intelligence.

(2) As an abstract noun to denote the state of being intelligent, intelligence is real enough, in much the same way as success and productivity and happiness are real. No-one would deny that it is helpful to describe one person as being more intelligent than another, when referring to their capabilities at mental tasks, and an indication of a person's intelligence level can be a useful item of information. There is nothing objectionable about saying that someone possesses high intelligence when that term is introduced simply as an alternative way of stating that the person is highly intelligent. Used in this way, a

person's intelligence level is an indication of the output or product of that individual's activities; it tells us how the person performs.

Similarly, there is nothing intrinsically objectionable about designating someone who is more intelligent than another as having higher intelligence. To say that someone has high intelligence could be regarded as simply a way of indicating that he or she belongs within the category of people who are highly intelligent. Introduced in that way, saying 'she did well because she had enough intelligence' would amount to no more than saying something like 'He failed because he is a loser' or 'Her film was a hit because she's a big success.'

However, in the following, third, sense of the word, the existence of intelligence is more questionable.

(3) The third common use of the word goes beyond *describing* what is achieved, and rather than just referring to the product of someone's mental activities also implies that they are being explained. Introducing an abstract noun as an alternative way of depicting a state of affairs originally described by an adjective (as in the change from 'she is intelligent' to 'she has intelligence') carries certain dangers. In particular, there is a common tendency to 'reify' concepts, and assume that if the noun exists there must also exist some corresponding concrete underlying thing or event. At the same time, it tends to be wrongly assumed that such a noun must indicate the cause or reason for a state of affairs, rather than simply describing something. It is frequently inferred, for example, that the concept of intelligence does not merely describe what a person can do, compared with others, but points to the reason why. That usage is evident in statements such as 'she did well because she had enough intelligence', or 'it was his high intelligence that made him a powerful thinker'.

It is when intelligence is introduced as a concept that is intended to be genuinely explanatory that its legitimacy becomes questionable and the question of whether intelligence exists needs raising. The limitations of this concept of intelligence are illustrated by looking at another familiar concept that has similar limitations, productivity. As we observed, productivity, like intelligence, is a useful term for a number of practical purposes. It makes sense to say that one factory is more productive than another, and assessments of productivity enable helpful predictions to be made. But once we start to apply the concept of productivity as a means of explaining events or identifying their causes, its emptiness is apparent; saying 'my factory does well because it is productive' actually explains nothing. That is because a statement about productivity is a statement about outcomes, products, results, achievements or performances, and not a statement identifying a quality or process that underlies those outcomes. Consequently, a 'productivity theory' would be treated with some scepticism, if the author claimed that knowing about productivity would allow a person to understand how and why factories differ in their output. And if that claim to wisdom was being made by an author whose background experience was in developing productivity tests, and had little or no knowledge about how factories actually work and how goods are made in them, readers would be entitled to be even more sceptical.

With intelligence, those circumstances are paralleled alarmingly closely. As we shall discover in later chapters, despite the presumptions of intelligence theorists there is no convincing reason for assuming that anything is genuinely explained by the concept of intelligence.

In the chapter that follows we turn to a practical question: 'Is intelligence changeable?' The answer to that has important implications for real-life issues, and it also has a bearing upon the possible role of Spearman's g factor. If that general factor is a genuinely important influence on a person's intelligence level, a consequence would be that IQ scores are largely unchangeable. Conversely, the discovery that people's IQs can readily alter would weaken the case for differences in g as a fundamental cause of variability in intelligence.

3

Can IQ be Increased?

Can a person's intelligence be raised, and if so to how large an extent? In the face of what appears to be irrefutable evidence that children's intelligence can be substantially increased, intelligence theorists continue to insist that a person's level of intelligence is stable and resistant to change. Arthur Jensen's well-known 1969 statement that 'compensatory education has been tried and it apparently has failed' has been reiterated by a number of authors of books published in the 1990s. Christopher Brand asserts that Jensen has been vindicated and that the impact of intervention programmes has been 'vanishingly slight' (1996: 134). J. Philippe Rushton believes that 'intelligence is the trait with the strongest stability over time' (1995: 24). Richard Herrnstein and Charles Murray say in *The Bell Curve* that 'the story of attempts to raise intelligence is one of high hopes, flamboyant claims, and disappointing results' (1994: 389). They claim that 'the more one knows about the evidence, the harder it is to be optimistic about prospects in the near future for raising the scores of the people who are most disadvantaged by their low scores' (1994: 390). Murray goes even further in a later publication, insisting that 'IQ can be raised with existing interventions only in modest amounts, inconsistently, and usually temporarily. . . . it is not yet clear that any intervention has yet demonstrated a long-term improvement in cognitive functioning' (1996: 145). The reason, he believes, is simply that 'an individual's realized intelligence, no matter whether realized through genes or the environment, is not very malleable' (1996: 150).

Much hinges on whether these assertions are true or false, because there are immense consequences. There are two crucial issues here. The first is the practical concern about the possibility of raising people's intelligence. One of *The Bell Curve's* main conclusions is that it is simply not worth trying to make people more intelligent, because for all practical purposes that just cannot be done. Or as the authors put it, 'the goal of raising intelligence among school-age children more than modestly, and doing so consistently and affordably, remains out of reach' (Herrnstein and Murray, 1994: 402). That argument, with all its pessimistic implications, will be hard to refute if it turns out that it genuinely is very difficult to raise someone's intelligence, as the *The Bell Curve* repeatedly insists, or if a person's intelligence can only be increased to a strictly limited extent, as Arthur Jensen claims. But if the facts contradict the belief that IQs are largely unchangeable, there is everything to be said for investing in educational programmes designed to raise intelligence, especially in children and young people. Limited intelligence is associated with many social problems, with people with low IQs experiencing all kinds of difficulties. So if we do discover that efforts to make young people more intelligent really can succeed, it will be impossible to justify any civilized society's neglecting to take the appropriate steps.

The second issue hinging on the changeability of intelligence concerns the assertion that the qualities reflected in an IQ test score have some kind of special status, setting intelligence apart from the acquired mental skills and abilities that people gain as a result of experience and learning. As was explained in Chapter 2, a central belief among IQ experts in the psychometric tradition, from Charles Spearman onwards, has been that intelligence is an inherent quality of a person, and far more than a collection of acquired mental capabilities. Rather than just being another intellectual ability, a person's intelligence is believed to provide a basic aptitude to perform mental tasks, with the g factor that underlies intelligence taking the form of mental power or energy. Seen in this light, someone's intelligence level is not simply an expression of the degree to which that person is intelligent, but also the reason why he or she is intelligent. Those who subscribe to intelligence theory reject the possibility that the mental capabilities tapped by an IQ test are simply acquired knowledge and learned skills.

So the answer to the question of whether or not intelligence is alterable not only has important social implications, but will help to confirm or refute the claim that intelligence holds a special and distinctive status among human qualities. Evidence confirming the view that intelligence cannot be readily changed would be consistent with the belief that intelligence is a largely fixed inherent quality of a person, and not just a reflection of the various mental capabilities that someone has acquired. However, the discovery that IQ scores are *not* unalterable and *can* be considerably improved would make that view hard to sustain. Should it turn out that, far from being fixed, the qualities assessed in an IQ test can be just as readily extended as those mental abilities that are known to be gained through an individual's experiences, it would be difficult to continue insisting that there is something particularly distinct or special about the capacities that are called upon when a person takes an IQ test. IQ scores would still be potentially useful, because they could still provide a useful sampling of someone's intellectual abilities, and therefore a helpful guide to that person's likely level of performance at problems requiring mental competence. But the argument that a person's IQ provides an indication of an underlying inherent faculty that provides the power or energy determining mental capacity would be badly dented.

Evidence That IQ Can Change

Is intelligence changeable or not? This question can only be answered after examining the relevant facts, which take the form of evidence from scientific investigations. Several sources of information have yielded relevant data concerning the changeability of human intelligence. First, there are studies of the consequences of being adopted. A number of investigations have examined the effects of adoption on a child's IQ. Evidence showing that these can be large would prove that intelligence can change substantially. Secondly, numerous studies have assessed the influence on IQ of educational intervention programmes designed to provide compensatory training for young children from poor home backgrounds. Thirdly, investigations have examined the possible effects on intelligence of variations in the amount of schooling that children receive. Fourthly, some research studies have looked at evidence suggesting that in certain nations people's average IQ levels may have altered from one generation to another. Finally, findings from a variety of other investigations have provided further information bearing on this issue.

Adoption Studies

Investigations of the consequences for a child of being adopted provide useful information about the effects on children of major changes in their everyday lives. If intelligence is largely fixed, the effects of adoption will be small, even if it takes place when a child is very young and the environment provided by the adopted home is very different from the child's former home background. But if intelligence can be altered, early adoption ought to have a substantial effect on intelligence, especially when life in the new home provides richer or poorer learning experiences than the ones available in the child's previous home background. As a result, moving a child early in life from seriously deprived home circumstances to a life with adoptive parents who are committed to giving plenty of support and stimulation might have a large influence on the child's intelligence.

Studies of adoption that are entirely satisfactory as research investigations are fairly rare. One reason for that is that the typically unhappy circumstances that lead to a child being adopted are not ones in which IQ testing is likely to have been conducted. Another complication is that because the troubled family circumstances preceding adoption can involve abuse or neglect of the child, and there may be a long period of instability, the child's capacity to gain from the improved circumstances of the new home may be reduced. Any newly adopted child will have to go through the difficult process of adapting to an unfamiliar life with new parents, and dealing with the residue of problems created by a child's previous experiences may consume much emotional energy.

Despite these difficulties, a number of investigations have provided evidence of adoption having had a large influence on children's intelligence. In the majority of studies the IQs of adopted children have been found to be above-average, contrasting with the typically below-average intelligence of their parents (Locurto, 1990). For instance, in a widely cited adoption study by Marie Skodak and Harold Skeels which was published in 1949, the IQs of the adopted children in adolescence were 21 points above those of their biological mothers (107 versus 86). Some of the biological mothers in the study were judged to be 'mentally defective', with an estimated average IQ of 63, and yet their children's average IQs were 96, over 30 points higher.

It is clear that for these children the change to a superior family environment produced dramatic gains in intelligence. Another finding was that the children of more intelligent biological parents were found to have higher IQs than the others, averaging 118. This is consistent with a strong genetic influence, but there are other possible reasons, one being that there was selective placement into adoptive homes, with the children of the more intelligent biological mothers being brought up in homes which were rated by the researchers as being superior on all the observed indications of their quality as learning environments. Another contributing factor is that the children probably differed in the quality of their prenatal environments and in the responsiveness of the parents in the period immediately following birth and prior to the infants being separated from their mothers. For these reasons the real contribution of genetic influences is hard to estimate.

The study by Skodak and Skeels provided clear evidence that being adopted can have a large influence on a child's intelligence. Similarly, in a more recent investigation Sandra Scarr discovered that the IQ scores of black children adopted by white parents were higher than the average scores of white children living in the same area (Rushton, 1995: 247). And in an adoption study conducted in Europe by Michel Schiff and his colleagues the average IQs of adopted children of working-class biological parents were found to be about 16 points higher than the average IQs of their biological siblings and half-siblings (Schiff et al., 1982).

In yet another study (Capron and Duyme, 1989) there was found to be an IQ difference averaging 12 points between adopted children, corresponding to differences in the socioeconomic levels of the adopting parents. There was a positive outcome of being reared in a socially advantaged rather than a disadvantaged adoptive home both for those children whose biological parents were from a low social class and for those whose biological parents' social level was higher. The 12-point difference between IQs of children reared by advantaged families compared with poorer families was roughly the same as the difference between the children of advantaged and disadvantaged biological parents. This finding indicates that in the children studied by Capron and Duyme the effects on IQ of differing post-adoptive experiences were at least as large as those differences in IQ that could be attributed to biological differences between the children, even if potentially important environmental influences such as the effects of the children's prenatal environments and their lives prior to adoption are discounted. Since there were no measures of the children's IQs prior to adoption in the study by Capron and Duyme, we cannot be certain to what extent intelligence increased as a consequence of the experience of being brought up in an advantaged family environment, but even *The Bell Curve*'s authors, Richard Herrnstein and Charles Murray, agree that the findings imply that moving to a good home environment can produce a benefit of almost 20 IQ points. Schiff and Lewontin (1986) compared the IQs of children whose origins were socially disadvantaged but were brought up in advantaged adoptive or fostering families with the IQs of their half-brothers and half-sisters who were reared in the home of the biological family. They, too, reported a 12-point improvement in IQ, providing further evidence of the substantial effects on intelligence of changing the environments in which children are reared.

In summary, investigations studying the effects of adoption on children's intelligence have yielded evidence suggesting that early adoption can result in substantial gains, averaging as much as 20 points in some circumstances.

Intervention Studies

Large IQ gains have also been reported in a number of studies that were conducted in order to evaluate programmes designed to equip children from disadvantaged home environments with knowledge and skills that a young person requires in order to take full advantage of the learning experiences provided at school. A survey of the earlier studies found that improvements averaged around seven IQ points over a six-month period.[1] Gains of a similar magnitude were reported following a careful analysis of the findings of 11 more recent studies of preschool education (Lazar and Darlington, 1982). Much larger improvements in intelligence had been reported in a major study by Bernadine Schmidt, who observed that the average IQs of severely disadvantaged adolescents attending an intensive three-year programme rose from 52 to 72.[2] Her investigation was criticized on a number of counts (see Locurto, 1991), but the main findings appear to be genuine.

Beginning in the 1960s, a substantial number of intervention programmes were financed by Project Head Start, an American initiative designed to provide opportunities for hundreds of thousands of young children living in poverty. Head Start programmes varied considerably in length, intensity, and effectiveness. Some provided a whole year of intensive learning experiences supervised by well-trained teachers. Others were much briefer and were poorly organized, and conducted by unqualified staff. It is therefore hardly surprising that the effectiveness of Head Start in improving children's intelligence varied from programme to programme. All the same, a substantial number of the projects resulted in impressive gains in IQ scores, sometimes as much as 10 points in a single summer (Zigler and Muenchow, 1992). One of the better Head Start interventions, known as the Perry Preschool Program, provided special education for three- and four-year-olds on five half-days per week for periods of up to two years. It led to IQ gains of 11 points, compared with the scores obtained by children in a control group, made up of comparable children who were given no special training. Even larger gains, averaging as much as 25 IQ points, were seen in a programme known as the Milwaukee Project, which provided daily care for the children of poor mothers with low IQs, as well as support for the mothers. The effects were long-lasting, with participants who had reached the age of 12 years still outscoring children in a comparison group by 10 IQ points.

Further impressive gains were obtained in an intensive long-term programme known as the Abecedarian Project, which was conducted in North Carolina (Ramey et al., 1984). This project gave children who came from deprived environments and were considered to be at high risk for retardation, enrichment and special care, from soon after birth until the age of five. Emphasis was placed on ensuring that the mothers were closely

involved in their child's early education. There were very substantial improvements, with the average IQ scores of the children who took part in the programme being 98 compared with
an average score of 90 in children forming a control group. The
advantages were still being maintained some years after the
intervention. For example, at the age of 12, 44 per cent of
children in a comparison group had IQs of less than 85, but this
was true of only 13 per cent of the participating children. Also,
whilst 55 per cent of the comparison group children had had to
repeat a grade, only 28 per cent of the children who participated
in the project did.

The success of the Abecedarian project led to the development
by Ramey and his colleagues of a further intervention programme for disadvantaged children, Project CARE. This placed
even more stress on the importance of working closely with each
child's family, but there was also a day-care component, beginning when the children were aged about three months (Wasik et
al., 1990). By the age of 24 months the IQs of the children who
participated in the programme by attending day-care classes
and receiving family support were 12 points above those of
children in a control group. Children whose families received
support aimed at encouraging parents to stimulate intellectual
development but who did not attend the day-care programme
showed no comparable gains. A possible reason was because the
level of support provided for the families, designed to help the
parents acquire and apply teaching skills, may have been
insufficient. It was based on infrequent visits to the homes,
averaging less than three per month. In other programmes,
visits to parents aimed at extending knowledge of children's
needs for good nutrition and mental stimulation have proved
effective for accelerating children's development even when
day-care programmes have not been provided (Wasik et al.,
1990).

Almost all the evidence from intervention studies concerning
the changeability of intelligence has taken the form of observed
increases in IQ. However, findings demonstrating that IQ can
also decline can provide equally valid evidence of its malleability. There is evidence of such declines in the reports of investigations studying the effects of reductions in schooling, described
in the following section. There are also some findings from other
investigations in which children's learning environments have

deteriorated rather than improved. For instance, Dennis and Dennis found that depriving infants of mental stimulation led to below-average scores on a number of tests of developmental progress (Dennis, 1941; Dennis and Dennis, 1951). Similarly, R.A. Spitz (1945) observed that the Developmental Quotients of infants who spent the first year of their life in an orphanage that provided minimal care declined from an average of 131 at the time the children were separated from their mothers, to 72. However, the scores of infants who spent their days in a nursery where their mothers were allowed to care for them did not decline at all.

Effects of Schooling

Investigations which have studied the effects of schooling on children's IQs have provided yet more evidence that intelligence levels can change. A number of studies assessing the influence of the summer vacation on IQ scores have shown decreases in children's intelligence during the summer vacation months, especially among those low-income youngsters whose summer activities were least likely to build on mental accomplishments acquired at school. Some interesting findings have emerged from a Swedish study which looked at the consequences for young people of dropping out of school. When comparisons were made between boys who were equated in IQ, socioeconomic status and school grades at age 13, those who dropped out had a loss of 1.8 IQ points on average for each year of high school not completed (Harnquist, 1968).

Studies relating IQ scores to the age of starting school have produced additional evidence that intelligence test scores are affected by the amount of schooling a child has received. An investigation conducted in West Germany exploited the fact that because children in the German school system were required to be six years of age by 1 April on the year of entering school, children whose birthdays were around that date could be very similar in age but have had up to a year's difference in schooling. It was found that those eight-year-olds who had received the most schooling were closer in mental abilities to the least schooled 10-year-olds than they were to the least

schooled eight-year-olds (Baltes and Reinert, 1969). Similar
findings were reported in a study conducted in Israel, where, as
in Germany, the fact that in any one school year there were
differences in children's ages made it possible to contrast the
effects of variations in the amount of schooling received when
age was kept constant with those of differences in age when
amount of schooling was constant (Cahan and Cohen, 1989).
The effects of differences in amount of schooling on children's
intellectual development were found to be about twice as large
as those of an equivalent difference in age. In another recent
study (Stelzl et al., 1995), it was found that schooling had
considerable effects on intelligence levels in 10-year-olds, and
that the influence of schooling extended to 'fluid' intelligence,
which is regarded by intelligence theorists as comprising the
aspects of intelligence that are most resistant to change. This
contradicts the claim of some researchers that schooling only
affects those ('crystallized') aspects of intelligence that are
acknowledged to be at least partly based on acquired knowledge.

A number of studies have demonstrated that missing school
is associated with low IQ, with the more the amount of schooling that is missed the bigger the drop. Michael Rutter and
Nicola Madge (1976) discovered that the forced closure of
schools as a consequence of wars or other major disruptions led
to decreases in IQ of around 5 points. Interpreting findings like
these is often difficult, because missing school is typically
associated with additional negative life events such as death of
a parent or other home problems. As a result, it is often not
clear whether or not the missed schooling is the main cause of
an observed deterioration in IQ scores. However, some of the
complications are less evident in American studies that were
conducted in remote communities in the Blue Ridge Mountains,
where from time to time the local schools stayed closed for
lengthy periods. For example, between 1918 and 1930 one
school in that region was open for only 16 months. Research
established that in circumstances like these the children who
had the most schooling had IQ advantages of 10–30 points
compared with children who had the least schooling. For instance, the IQs of children born in one community in 1940, who
had fairly regular schooling, averaged 11 points higher than

children born in the same community in 1930, who had substantially less schooling (Ceci, 1990; Sherman and Key, 1932; Tyler, 1965).

Similarly, depriving children of schooling as a consequence of the closure of some schools in Virginia during the 1960s (in an effort to prevent integration) had large negative effects, with the decreases in IQs averaging about 6 points per year of missed schooling.[3] Other investigations that were conducted in South Africa yielded comparable findings. For example, it was discovered that under circumstances in which schooling was cut short or delayed for reasons outside families' control, the earlier schooling began and the greater the amount of time spent attending school, the higher the children's IQ scores (Schmidt, 1966).

Generational Changes

Numerically, IQ scores stay roughly the same from one generation to another, but that apparent stability is artificial, and results from the fact that each time a test is modified or revised it is 'restandardized', with the average IQ score being reset to 100. That results in any real increases in average test performance becoming invisible. A series of investigations undertaken by James Flynn aimed at discovering what would have happened had the rescaling not taken place. In other words, if the same tests that people were taking, say, 50 years ago were still in use, what would have happened to people's IQ scores?

Flynn's investigations revealed that there have been surprisingly large changes, with real IQs steadily increasing, sometimes dramatically. For instance, in France between 1949 and 1974 there was an average gain of 21 IQ points, and in the Netherlands average scores gained 15.6 points in 18 years, and 8.7 points in the single decade between 1972 and 1982 alone (Flynn, 1987). There were comparable massive gains in Japan, Germany, and Austria, and smaller increases in Britain and the United States, with the average IQ improvement between 1950 and 1980 being 15 points. Flynn has pointed out that since there is no possible way in which genetic mechanisms can produce observable changes between one generation and the next, the causes must be entirely environmental. A number of

factors are likely to be involved, including the increasing complexity of life, better communications and more exposure to
information. Nutritional improvements may also have had an
influence.

Improved schooling is almost certainly one reason for the
changes; as Flynn noted, the average Dutch youngster who was
18 years old in 1982 had received two or three more years of
schooling than a comparable young person in 1972. However,
the improvements in intelligence cannot be explained away as
being merely in increase in narrow school-based skills. One
reason for being confident about this is the fact that there have
been large increases in scores at a variety of different tests.
Furthermore, Flynn has estimated that the direct effects of
improved schooling would have been small, as would the possible contribution of specific influences such as increased test
sophistication. Broader environmental factors appear to be the
main cause of the improvements (Flynn, 1991).

Other Evidence of the Malleability of Intelligence

A variety of investigations have produced further evidence
that a person's intelligence level can substantially change.
Some of these studies have examined the effects of physical
influences such as lead and alcohol (both of which can have
negative effects) rather than psychological causes of IQ
changes. There have also been a number of studies of the
consequences for IQ of prenatal and postnatal improvements
in nutrition. An investigation of Dutch males who had been
affected by prenatal malnutrition resulting from wartime
famine showed no long-term effects on intelligence (Stein et al.,
1975), but in a number of studies improvements in mental test
performance have been seen in undernourished children following the provision of dietary supplements.

The findings of some investigations suggest that improvements in diet may sometimes produce gains in intellectual
functioning even in children who are not seriously undernourished (Schoenthaler et al., 1991) but these findings have
been challenged (Sanders, 1992); other investigations have not
replicated the effects. Evidence from further investigations
indicates that either breast-feeding or adopting alternative

procedures which ensure that babies are given their mothers' milk can raise a child's intelligence, possibly by as much as 10 IQ points. However, the research into the possible effects of nutrition on intelligence is surrounded by controversy. One psychologist, Hans Eysenck (1992), has claimed that the evidence indicates that vitamin and mineral supplementation can improve IQ in a sizeable proportion of apparently adequately nourished children, but other researchers disagree. As an American Psychological Association task force concluded in 1996, 'the role of nutrition in intelligence remains obscure' (Neisser et al., 1996).

There is also evidence that common infections, which in some parts of the world affect many children, are associated with lowered performance at cognitive skills. Children who are successfully treated for such infections display cognitive gains, and a number of studies have demonstrated negative correlations between levels of mental skills and the presence of common infections (Nokes and Bundy, 1994). The precise nature of cause-and-effect relationships is not clear. It is possible that any effects of these infections are indirect rather than direct, affecting intelligence by preventing a child from attending school or making it less likely that a child at school will concentrate effectively on study tasks. However, it is clear that successful efforts to cure intestinal helminth infections can have the practical consequence of raising levels of children's performance at cognitive tasks, even though the precise reasons for this remain unclear.

Motivational influences can affect a person's IQ score. For instance, in one study it was found that giving black inner-city children tokens that could be exchanged for toys for each correct test response raised average scores by 13 points (Johnson et al., 1984). The tokens did not have comparable effects on middle-class children's scores, possibly because they, unlike the other children, were initially well motivated to do as well as they could at the test.

A number of studies have provided evidence that IQ scores can be increased, sometimes very considerably, by giving training that is closely related to the specific contents of test items (see, for example, Guinagh, 1971). Understandably enough, it has been objected that the gains achieved in such 'teaching to the test' coaching cannot be said to indicate genuine improvements in intelligence. However, it could be just as convincingly argued that the absence of a clear definition of intelligence that makes clear the nature of the abilities that need to be improved in order to raise intelligence creates unreasonable handicaps, adding to the difficulty of devising effective educational programmes for helping young people to become more intelligent. Because of this, even if it was discovered that efforts to add to the mental capacities that determine a person's IQ score were less successful than efforts to increase other human capabilities, that could be partly due to failure to specify the nature of the qualities that need to be acquired in order to increase a person's IQ score. It would certainly not prove that the qualities determining level of performance in an intelligence test are intrinsically any harder to extend than are other abilities.

Objections to the Findings Demonstrating IQ Increases

In the face of the large body of evidence from various sources demonstrating that IQs can and do change considerably, it might have been expected that psychometric writers on intelligence would have abandoned the belief that intelligence is largely unchangeable. Yet that has not happened. A frequent response, typified by that of the authors of *The Bell Curve*, has been to raise objections and criticisms which, it is claimed, nullify the research evidence. Two main objections have been raised, plus a number of additional criticisms.

The 'Fading' Objection

The first objection is that whilst it cannot be denied that a number of investigations have produced evidence of major gains in IQ, in a number of cases the improvements have not been permanent and have diminished over the years, in some instances to zero. The initial effects are said to 'fade' or 'wash out'. That demonstrates, it is argued, that changes in IQ can only be temporary rather than permanent, and that in practice intelligence remains largely fixed.

As a justification for refusing to abandon the belief that intelligence cannot be altered, that objection is unconvincing on a number of grounds. For a start, it applies to only some of the research findings. For instance, the evidence of inter-generational changes in measured intelligence is entirely untouched by the finding that fading can occur. So, too, are most of the findings of adoption studies. In other investigations it is clear that even when some fading has taken place substantial increases in IQ still remain.

But the main reason why the 'fading' objection is unconvincing is that, on the assumption that the kinds of expertise that determine a person's scores at an intelligence test are essentially acquired knowledge and skills rather than having the special status of inherent or unlearned qualities, there is every reason to expect them to fade, in some circumstances. It is an almost universal characteristic of acquired competences that when there is a prolonged absence of opportunities to use, practise, and profit from them, they do indeed decline. It would therefore be highly surprising if acquired gains in intelligence did *not* sometimes fade or diminish. Indeed, had the research findings showed that IQs never fade or decline, *that* evidence would have provided some support for the view that measured intelligence possesses the inherent – rather than acquired – status that intelligence theorists and other writers within the psychometric tradition have believed it to have. So evidence of fading improvements, far from forming support for the view that intelligence cannot change, actually provides additional evidence of its malleability.

In short, the fact that gains do sometimes fade or decline rather than invariably being permanent tends to refute rather than confirm the belief that intelligence is a special and largely unalterable human attribute. The only circumstance in which it might be reasonably predicted that gains in intelligence would never decline would be one in which the effects on intelligence of an early intervention were like those of a protective inoculation or 'shot in the arm'. But this analogy, which has been introduced from to time, has always been a totally inappropriate one, except in relation to the relatively small amount of research on the effects of interventions taking the form of improved nutrition or breast-feeding. The environmental influences that lead to mental abilities being increased are nothing like the processes that make inoculations effective. Enough is known about the processes of human development and learning for it to be certain that the mechanisms by which people acquire mental expertise are not even remotely akin to inoculations.

Why *does* fading take place? It is not hard to find reasons. There is every reason to suppose that for many young children whose IQ scores have increased after involvement in intervention programmes, the impoverished conditions of ghetto existence in communities often characterized by urban squalor, bad housing, substance abuse, violence and massive unemployment, with poor schooling and restricted family life, will give them few opportunities to use or extend their newly gained school-based skills and competences. Commenting on the schools attended by ex-Head Start programme children, researchers have observed that these are often unsafe and provide a far from stimulating educational climate, with low average achievements, restricted resources, and poor relationships between staff and students. In these circumstances it is almost inevitable that the new knowledge and skills that contributed to the gain in IQ will fade, for essentially the same reasons that most other acquired skills and competences decline when there is a lack of opportunities to practise them.

The findings of an investigation by Victoria Seitz demonstrate that the above account is more than just a plausible scenario (Zigler and Seitz, 1982). Seitz measured the effects of a four-year educational intervention programme emphasizing mathematical skills, in which inner-city boys participated, beginning in kindergarten. The programme was highly effective, but in a follow-up study, continued over several years, the large improvement in those boys who had taken part, compared with a control group, gradually diminished. At the end of the programme the boys who took part in it were two years ahead, but by the age of 15 or so they were only one year ahead.

Seitz took steps to find out why this fading was taking place. She found no evidence of a loss of basic mathematical ability, but she discovered that the older boys were simply not being taught the kinds of mathematical skills that they needed, if they were to maintain their high test scores. For instance, to score well at the achievement tests used with older children it is essential to have some knowledge of algebra and geometry, but Seitz found that while the majority of middle-class children were being taught these subjects, the disadvantaged pupils were not getting the necessary teaching. For that reason they could hardly be expected to do well. As Seitz perceived, the true picture was not one of fading ability but of diminishing use of it.

Despite all the negative influences which make it likely that those IQ gains that follow intervention programmes will tend to fade when children return to deprived circumstances in which they have few opportunities to apply their newly acquired mental abilities, there have been some intervention programmes in which fading has not occurred. One might expect that the writers of recent books on intelligence would have applauded the successful prevention of fading, but that has not happened. On the contrary, if fading is seen as an opportunity for making objections, absence of fading is seized upon as an alternative justification for criticism, a nice example of having it both ways. For example, Herman Spitz, after acknowledging the unarguable differences between experimental and control group IQs in the Abecedarian project, observes that 'the negligible additional effects after 4.5 more years in the programme should at least make one cautious about this kind of intervention's potential for permanently and appreciably modifying general intelligence' (1992: 235). In other words, he seems to be saying that even if the programme makes a substantial difference which does *not* fade, something must still be wrong with the programme. However large and stable the outcome, it cannot really be permanent unless it goes on increasing year after year, in the face of all the unfavourable circumstances of ghetto life. The logic of that argument is elusive.

The 'Failure' Objection

Another objection that has been introduced by some authors in order to justify a refusal to be convinced by the evidence that intelligence is changeable is that not all education interventions have produced big changes in IQ. That is certainly true, but as an argument that intelligence is fixed it falls short on three counts.

First, to claim that any failure to induce a change can be regarded as proof that changing is impossible is wrong for the same reason that claiming that an inability to discover a previously located remote island proves that it does not exist would be misguided. In each case, a failure to achieve a goal is being incorrectly used as evidence that the goal is unachievable. Even if it had been true that all brief intervention studies had failed to raise IQs, the case for IQ being unchangeable would not be entirely conclusive. Thirty years ago, the fact that short-lived efforts to increase people's memory spans had met with very limited success was widely believed to confirm the belief that a person's memory span was unchangeable. But in 1981, when William Chase and Anders Ericsson published the first of a series of findings demonstrating that highly motivated subjects who are trained over a period of a year or more can increase their memory spans by as much as a factor of 10, it immediately became evident that the prevailing view was misguided.

Secondly, at least some of the intervention studies that did not produce large improvements in measured intelligence (as well as some of those that did) were not specifically designed to change IQ, and in many cases they did achieve the intended benefits they were designed to achieve. Since IQ levels have sometimes been only weakly related to the main goals of an intervention programme, only by adopting a cart-before-the-horse line of reasoning could it be said that the failure of some of these studies to produce large IQ gains provides positive evidence of the unchangeability of intelligence.

The third – and most powerful – riposte to the criticism that not all interventions have produced large gains relates to the duration and intensity of compensatory educational experiences that have been provided in intervention programmes. It revolves around the question of how much time needs to be devoted to improving IQ scores in order to make a substantial difference. If we start by assuming that the skills that contribute to a person's IQ scores have no special or unlearned status, and are acquired by processes that are similar to the ones involved in the acquisition of other kinds of mental expertise, then it makes sense to ask how much time is typically needed in order to gain those mental abilities that are acknowledged to be acquired through learning. This knowledge can provide a guide to the amount of time that would be expected to be necessary in order to make big gains in IQ.

Learning always does take time, especially when broad varieties of expertise are involved. In music, for example, it takes a young performing instrumentalist about 3,500 hours, on average, to reach the standard of a good amateur musician (Grade Eight of the board examinations conducted in Britain). That assumes that the individual is well motivated, is given sufficient individual instruction by an expert, and practises conscientiously (Sloboda et al., 1996). A considerably longer period of training, around 10,000 hours, is required in order to reach professional standards. Broadly comparable amounts of training and practice are needed in order to reach high levels of expertise in other skill areas such as chess and various sports. Mastery of a foreign language similarly necessitates periods of learning that stretch into thousands of hours.

In the case of an IQ test performance, since a wide range of knowledge and skills is being sampled, it would appear reasonable to suppose that the periods of special training needed in order to produce major improvements would be at least as large as the amounts of time necessary for reaching high degrees of expertise in narrower areas of expertise such as music, chess, and sports. In other words, in order for a well-designed programme to make a major impact a duration of at least several thousand hours would seem to be needed. Only if a number of competently designed programmes that were at least as substantial as that failed to make an impact on IQ would there be any genuine grounds for concluding that the knowledge and skills assessed in intelligence tests are more resistant to change than are other varieties of competence.

In fact, however, the majority of the programmes that have been evaluated in order to assess their effects on children's IQs have been of short duration. Very few have involved anything like the amount of instruction and practice that is acknowledged to be necessary even in narrower skill areas such as music. Consider, for instance, a typical one-summer Head Start programme lasting for 10 weeks, with three two-hour sessions per week. Here the total investment for each child is no more than 60 hours, a period of time that is not even remotely comparable to the lengthy durations mentioned above. And yet at the time Arthur Jensen made his confident and hugely influential comment that compensatory education had failed, and insisted that there had been a uniform failure of compensatory programmes wherever they had been tried, more than half of the Head Start programmes he was so sweepingly dismissing had been interventions lasting no more than two months. Not until three years later, in 1972, did it become customary to have programmes which extended to a whole year.

Even with considerably longer and more intense projects than the ones in use at the time Jensen made his criticisms, such as a programme that lasted for 40 weeks with five six-hour instructional periods per week, the total time involved would be only 1,200 hours. As we have seen, that is considerably less than the durations of training necessary in order to gain real expertise at particular skills. For a four-and-a-half-year-old living in an impoverished home environment that provided few opportunities for the child to practise or develop the new cognitive skills outside the periods of attendance at the programme, that impressive-sounding 1,200 hours would represent no more than about 6 per cent of the child's waking time since birth.

This seems hardly enough to make a major impact on the totality of a young person's experience. It is puny in relation to the actual differences in everyday experiences that are seen to accompany real differences in young children's capabilities. For instance, in an observational study of child language that was conducted by Betty Hart and Todd Risley (1995) in order to cast light on the finding that three-year-olds from different social classes vary in the size of their spoken vocabularies, it was discovered that in a typical week the number of words children experienced differed by as much as 150,000. By the age of three, children in professional families had heard more than 30 million words. In contrast, children from working-class families and families on welfare had heard around 20 million and 10 million words respectively. These data make it clear that underlying the observed variations in children's language skills were huge and long-lasting differences in their language experiences. The fact that large IQ gains have been produced in some intervention studies, in spite of the fact that the impact of the compensatory experiences on the children's lives did not even approach this magnitude, seems to provide rather conclusive evidence that IQ scores are indeed highly changeable.

Taking into account the restricted durations of Head Start programmes, as well as the fact that the majority of them have involved group rather than individual instruction, often by teachers who were not highly qualified or experienced, some of the gains in IQ have been remarkably impressive by any standards. In the face of that evidence, even if we were to set aside the further support for the view that intelligence is changeable that is contributed by a substantial body of findings from quite different sources, the belief that intelligence is largely unchangeable appears extremely hard to justify.

The 'Intelligence is Stable' Objection

Another possible objection is that since measured intelligence displays considerable stability, even in children, with correlations in scores from one year to the next averaging around .80, it must be largely fixed and unchangeable. It cannot be denied that intelligence does indeed tend to remain stable, at least in the restricted sense that most young people's IQ scores do not wildly change from one year to the next. However, that fact has little or no bearing on the question of its capacity to change.

Consider certain other stable characteristics, such as a person's address or telephone number. These, in common with IQ, tend to remain the same from one year to the next. But they do so not because they are unchangeable but because of a variety of reasons that encourage people to go on living in the same house. No-one would claim that the fact that addresses and telephone numbers tend not to change very often means that they *cannot* be changed, and people do change their addresses and telephone numbers whenever there are adequate reasons for that to happen.

Another reason for pointing out that evidence of the stability of intelligence provides no support for the view that it is unchangeable lies in the fact that a child's IQ is only stable from around the age of five. That is to say, intelligence levels only become stable after the enormous differences that are found in children's experiences, culture, and environment have already had considerable time to exert their effects. Had it been the case that the stability of intelligence was an indication that it was unchangeable, intelligence would be stable from the earliest years of life.

Finally, it is worth noting, that, as *The Bell Curve*'s authors appreciate, but some other writers on intelligence do not, the finding that a trait may be largely inherited does not mean that it is unchangeable, and the fact that a trait is hard to change does not mean that it is inherited.

The 'IQ is Not Really Intelligence' Objection

Yet another objection, and one that has sometimes been raised as a response to demonstrations of large IQ gains resulting from intervention studies, is that increases in IQ are not necessarily increases in 'real' intelligence, and may be no more than improvements in test scores.

If it was advanced consistently, that argument might have some merit. However, it is not used consistently. For instance, those who introduce such an argument never apply it in order to support the view that 'fading' or 'wash-out' effects do not indicate 'real' decrements in intelligence, although that would be quite a reasonable view to hold, especially since in a number of the studies in which fading has taken place children have continued to show other kinds of gains that point to increases in intelligence, such as improved school performance. Indeed, there is strong evidence that impressive school attainments and other indications of intellectual ability can be unaccompanied by high IQ scores. In particular, as James Flynn (1991) has shown, the intellectual achievements of Americans with Asian origins are very often much better than would be predicted on the basis of their IQ scores.

So although a case can be made for the view that there are important aspects of intelligence that are not measured in intelligence tests, it is significant that the argument is only selectively and inconsistently advanced by those who wish to dismiss observed IQ gains contradicting the belief that intelligence cannot be altered. If those writers were to truly acknowledge the force of the case that there are aspects of intelligence that are not reflected in IQ scores, they would also have to concede that the findings of those intervention studies in which

IQ gains have been relatively small or have faded may not, after all, be indicative of a failure to induce permanent gains in a person's real intelligence.

There is a tendency for writers who insist that IQ scores are reliable indicators of intelligence to hold to that view when it suits their argument to do so, but change their position when it is more convenient to do that. For example, in Christopher Brand's 1996 book *The* g *Factor: General Intelligence and its Implications*, the author vigorously defends IQ tests in Chapter 1, examining some criticisms that he calls 'six proposed escape routes from admitting that IQ tests measure intelligence' and concluding that they 'all turn out to be blind alleys'. But by Chapter 4, the IQ improvements resulting from a number of intervention studies are suddenly seen to be highly suspect as indicators of genuine intelligence. At that point the author notes, for example, that

> like any measuring device, an IQ test can be made to give a reading that no longer reflects what it is intended to measure . . . IQ scores can increase under unusual procedures; but wider and lasting educational gains can hardly be expected if no real and lasting gain has occurred in underlying mental ability: It was just such gains that eluded Head Start programmers. Even in the thorough and well-documented Abecedarian Project, gains on a particular test – whether the gains were great or, more usually, small – were not reflected in IQ assessments on different tests at later ages, or in school skills. Such learning as the children had shown was 'shallow' and did not transfer. (p. 132)

So for Brand the same IQ scores that were heralded and defended in his first chapter as being the surest and most reliable possible indicators of a person's intelligence have become, by Chapter 4, totally unreliable. But by the end of the same chapter the author has changed tack once again. Suddenly, IQ has once more become respectable, being, Brand insists, 'just as important and predictive for children as are their first early attainments'. And 'notions of IQ's "unimportance"' are once again sharply attacked (p. 145).

Brand is far from being the only writer on intelligence to be two-faced about the validity of IQ scores as indicators of intelligence. Even the authors of *The Bell Curve*, who strenuously argue in favour of IQ scores as the best available indicators of intelligence and throughout their book rarely hesitate to assume that differences in IQ scores reflect real differences in intelligence, alter their position in order to criticize the success-ful Abecedarian project on the grounds that the high IQ scores gained by children under the age of three in that study 'are poor predictors of later intelligence test scores' (Herrnstein and Murray, 1994: 407), while choosing not to make that point in relation to any of the numerous other research findings in their book to which it could equally well be applied.

Conclusion

There exists a large amount of convincing evidence that a person's intelligence level can alter, sometimes very substan-tially. None of the objections that have been raised by psycho-logists who have been unwilling to accept this evidence are convincing. Like other broadly based mental skills and capabil-ities, the ones that are assessed in mental tests are not acquired quickly or without effort, but there is no firm basis for claiming that the capacities that determine someone's intelligence test score are distinct from other acquired capabilities, either in being more fundamental or in being inherent attributes of the person, let alone in being immutable.

It is important to remember that in addition to its implica-tions concerning the real nature of human intelligence, the evidence that intelligence levels can substantially change has a strong bearing on social policy. Proponents of intelligence theory, such as the authors of *The Bell Curve*, have coupled their conviction that intelligence cannot be improved with the observation that adults with low IQs tend to get into difficulties, experience poverty and joblessness, and become inadequate parents, to arrive at the pessimistic conclusion that nothing can be done about those social problems that are related to low IQ. As we have seen, it is claimed that advanced societies have no alternative but to acquiesce in the growth of a permanent underclass, made up of unintelligent individuals who are cut off from the prosperity and the opportunities that educated people in steady employment take for granted.

If it were true that intelligence is unchangeable, there might be some basis for believing in such a grim prospect. But, as we have seen in this chapter, intelligence is not at all unchangeable. It can be increased, and very substantially. Doing that on a large scale takes resources, of course, but the task can be done. The enormous gains that would follow would almost certainly outweigh the costs.

In a prosperous society, only a self-fulfilling prophecy resulting from widespread acceptance of the false visions expounded by those who refuse to see that intelligence is changeable would enable the perpetuation of a permanent caste of people who are prevented from acquiring the capabilities evident in successful men and women and sharing their rewards. Unfortunately, however, at present just that set of circumstances appears to be in place. Underclasses do not emerge for no reason; they are created by unequal societies. While severe social deprivation persists, widespread low intelligence may seem inevitable. As we have seen in this chapter, however, a solid mass of hard evidence demonstrates that the apparent inevitability is a sham.

Notes

1. See Snow and Yalow (1982) for a survey of early investigations.
2. Schmidt's investigations are discussed by Locurto (1991).
3. Investigation by R.L. Green et al., cited by Neisser et al. (1996).

4

Race and Intelligence

When the forces of the German Third Reich invaded Lithuania in June 1941 they took with them special squads known as 'Einsatzgruppen' – or 'Action Groups'. These men were responsible for the job of murdering, by shooting or gassing, any political commissars who fell into the army's hands, as well as intellectuals and Gypsies, and, especially, all Jews they could find. The Einsatzgruppen had made elaborate arrangements for their killing operations, but on arrival in Lithuania they discovered that a group of anti-Soviet 'partisans' had already launched a large-scale pogrom against the Jews, beginning their killings of men, women, and children the moment the German invasion began. The Germans were quick to take advantage of this situation, organizing 8,400 of the killers into groups of volunteers, and with their cooperation the ghastly crime of slaughtering virtually all of Lithuania's quarter of a million Jews was completed by the end of the year. This turn of events was far from unique. In the other Baltic countries, and also the Ukraine, the invading Germans encountered large numbers of savagely anti-Semitic local inhabitants who rushed at the opportunity to kill Jews (Sereny, 1995).

That is what racism means. It begins, as Gitta Sereny has written, with a feeling of physical or intellectual rejection of a human being who is seen as different from oneself. It can take many forms, ranging from Hitler's passionate hatred of the Jews to the villager's fear and loathing of the tribe on the other side of the river and to the xenophobe's virulent distrust of anyone outside the circle made up of those who are 'one of us'. For the racist only some people are regarded as fully fledged individuals. The remainder are at best the inhabitants of an outgroup made up of those who do not belong to one's own people and with whom one does not fully identify. At worst they are the 'Untermenschen' – underclass – targeted in the 1943 statement of Nazi Reichskommissar in the Ukraine Erich Koch that 'We are a master race, which must remember that the lowliest German worker is racially and biologically a thousand times more valuable than the population here' (Sereny, 1995: 311). The cancer of racism is still alive and well, as recent massacres in Bosnia, Rwanda, Uganda, Nigeria, Iraq, Cambodia, Indonesia, and many other places demonstrate all too clearly.

It is important to keep facts like these in mind when confronting the work of present-day psychologists who, like the Nazi scientists of the 1930s, claim that the study of race differences is a purely 'objective' and 'scientific' enterprise. As was mentioned in Chapter 2, racist thinking was common among the early developers of intelligence testing. Perhaps surprisingly, a strong interest in racial variations in intelligence is still evident in the work of a number of scholars. The most recent theory in this tradition is that of J. Philippe Rushton, who has written extensively on race and intelligence. His 1995 book *Race, Evolution, and Behavior* claims that there are substantial differences in the intelligence of different racial groups which can only be explained from an evolutionary perspective. Rushton, a professor of psychology at the University of Western Ontario, in Canada, whose published statements include the assertion that Nazi Germany's military prowess was connected to the purity of its gene pool, believes that social scientists who object to his views are guilty of an absurd adherence to political correctness.

Another psychologist, Christopher Brand, of the University of Edinburgh, had his book *The g Factor* withdrawn by its publishers (John Wiley and Sons) shortly after its publication in 1996 when they discovered that the book contained views that they found repellent. Brand believes that 'It is a scientific fact that black Americans are less intelligent than white Americans and the IQ of Asians is higher than blacks' (quoted in Bell, 1996). He is convinced that different races are intellectually unequal, insisting that while Hong Kong is as advanced as many western cities, 'Africa, however, remains the utterly dark continent' (quoted in Bell, 1996).

Professor Richard Lynn of the University of Ulster holds similar views about intelligence, and is one of the mercifully few university scholars to favour the practice of 'eugenics', which involves the selective breeding of humans. He has written that people who are poor or ill 'are weak specimens whose proliferation needs to be discouraged in the interests of the improvement of the genetic quality of the group' (quoted in Lane 1995: 129), a point of view that has been almost universally condemned ever since the activities of the Nazi regime in Germany made it evident just what it implied in practice. Lynn asserts that only the Caucasoid and the Mongoloid races have made any significant contribution to civilization (quoted in Rosen and Lane, 1995: 59). But in the view of Leon Kamin, a strong critic of the psychometric approach to intelligence, Lynn's reporting of research by other investigators examining the mental abilities of Africans was inaccurate to the extent that 'Lynn's distortions and misrepresentations of the data constitute a truly venomous racism, combined with scandalous disregard for scientific objectivity' (1995: 86).

Both Rushton and Lynn have been extensively funded by an organization known as the Pioneer Fund, which was founded in 1916 with the support of Madison Grant, the author of a book entitled *The Passing of the Great Race, or The Racial Basis of European History*, and a supporter of the eugenics movement as well as a promoter of Nazi racial propaganda in America. The fund's first president, Harry Laughlin, was another enthusiast for eugenics, who pushed through legislation blocking entry to the United States of Jews fleeing pogroms in Russia and developed a programme that resulted in the forced sterilization of thousands of American people. Its treasurer, John B. Trevor, worked for a group that was named in a United States Justice Department sedition indictment for pro-Nazi activities, and in 1962 called for the release of all Nazi war criminals and announced its support for South Africa's 'well-reasoned racial policy' of apartheid (Miller, 1995). The Pioneer Fund supports research into racial differences, and has given grants to people such as William Shockley, who proposed a fund to pay 'intellectually inferior' individuals to be sterilized, with the fee increasing by $1,000 for each IQ point below 100 (Sedgwick, 1995), and Ralph Scott, an ex vice-president of the pro-Nazi German–American National Congress, who used Pioneer money to oppose busing. Other recipients of the fund's support include a University of Southern Mississippi professor who was arrested for mail fraud in 1966 after a raid on his home in which police found a cache of weapons, Nazi memorabilia, and large quantities of racist, anti-Semitic, and anti-Catholic literature (Miller, 1995).

If it were not for the fact that others have been influenced by them, the extreme views of the above-mentioned individuals could be ignored. However, the writers of the highly influential *The Bell Curve* drew heavily on their research and views. Herrnstein and Murray acknowledge that they 'benefited especially' from the advice of Lynn. They attach much importance to a paper by him on race differences in intelligence that was published in *Mankind Quarterly*, an anthropology journal that concentrates on racial differences and has been denounced by mainstream anthropologists. It was founded by a Scottish white supremacist and is financed by the Pioneer Fund. *The Bell Curve*'s senior author, Richard Herrnstein, is thanked by Rushton for giving advice on drafts of *Race, Evolution, and Behavior*, and Herrnstein and Murray return the favour by praising, in *The Bell Curve*, his 'detailed and convincing empirical reports of the race differences' (Herrnstein and Murray, 1994: 643).

Rushton's Theory

Seizing on the observation in a number of studies that the average intelligence test scores of black and white people differ by around 10 IQ points, Rushton is convinced that the explanation lies in the existence of genetic differences between races, and his theory purports to explain their origins. Rushton starts by dividing the population of the world into three racial categories: Caucasoid, Mongoloid, and African. (This division conveniently ignores a number of complications such as the fact that anthropologists question the scientific legitimacy of race as a category, and the finding that differences between individuals within races are as large as differences between races. Rushton also ignores the problem that many millions of individuals, including much of the population of South America, belong in none of these categories, as well as the awkward fact that race is a social construct rather than a biological unit.)

Rushton's theory asserts that evolution has provided the reason for people in the three races he designates apparently differing in intelligence. The explanation, according to him, is straightforward. About 200,000 years ago, African man emerged

from the ancestral *homo* line, and subsequently there were
further divisions, between Africans and non-Africans about
100,000 years ago and between Caucasoids and Mongoloids
about 40,000 years ago. Those people who migrated out of Africa
into the colder climates of Europe and Asia encountered more
challenging environments. As a result, they were more
stringently selected for intelligence, forward planning, and
sexual and personal restraint. Selection also favoured, to a
greater extent in Caucasoids and Mongoloids compared with
Africans, a parenting strategy that involved having relatively
small numbers of infants and investing a relatively large
amount of care and attention in them. The selective pressures
favouring high intelligence were at their strongest among the
groups of people living in Siberia.

That, in essence, is the theory, and Rushton believes it to be
true and expects his readers to take it seriously. It is worth
reminding ourselves that some scholars do indeed take Rushton's views very seriously. Richard Lynn, for example, agrees
with *The Bell Curve*'s authors' view and describes the book (on
the cover blurb) as 'A major synthesis of social science and
evolutionary theory on the issue of race differences in intelligence and behavior.' Other scientists, including Arthur Jensen, Hans Eysenck, and Thomas Bouchard, have offered similar
words of approval.

Not everyone is so enthusiastic, however. As Alan Goodman
observes,

> Rushton's key contribution to science, I suggest, is a thermo-
> dynamic theory of evolution. One can either have sexual potency or
> smarts; it is either a big brain or a big penis. One could use race as
> a social variable to begin to get at the influences of sociopolitical and
> economic processes on IQ scores, but to go on to use this social
> category as biology and to discuss separate evolutions moves into
> the realm of fiction. (1996: 164)

Criticisms and Counter-arguments

There are two fatal flaws in the theory. First, from an anthropo-
logical viewpoint it makes no sense at all. Until about 10,000
years ago the extent to which human survival depended upon
intelligent problem solving seems to have been essentially the
same throughout the inhabited world, as is apparent from the

fact that the same tools have been found to be in use at any one
time from one end of the world to the other. It was only when
farming started to develop, within the past 10,000 years or so,
that the kinds of changes occurred that could have meant
higher intelligence having greater survival value in some
groups of humans than in others. But that is far too short a
period for evolutionary processes to create changes in attributes
that have as complex a genetic background as intelligence and
thinking capacities do (Brace, 1996). In any case, natural selection tends to reduce genetic variation in traits that contribute to
survival. Therefore, if Rushton's theory was correct there would
be considerably decreased variability in Caucasoids and Mongoloids, compared with Africans, in those traits that he claims
to have been subject to natural selection in the former two
racial groups but not in the latter. There is no evidence that this
is so. It is of course true that there are differences between
human groups in reproduction rates and in the degree to which
parents involve themselves with their children. However, these
are largely a consequence of differing social and economic
conditions and differences between social groups in cultural
traditions, values, and educational opportunities. In my grand-
parents' generation families of 10 children were commonplace,
but no-one argues that it is evolution that has caused people
today to have smaller families.

The second flaw in Rushton's theory resides in the fact that in
order to manufacture an explanatory theory that intends to
account for the supposedly genetic differences in the intelligence of people from different racial origins, he has had to
ignore a number of inconvenient facts about genetics. Measures
of heritability only tell us the contribution made by genetics to
the observed variation of a trait or attribute within a particular
population living within a particular environment. Because of
that, all indications of the heritability of a human trait are
specific to certain groups living at a particular time in certain
environments. Heritability estimates based on one population
or group cannot be applied to another. Moreover, even when a
trait has a large genetic component, the differences between
groups in that trait may be caused entirely by environmental
influences. For instance, height has a high genetic component
and yet the reason why height varies considerably from one
population to another is largely the result of environmental

influences such as health and nutrition (Alland, 1996). In short, the fact that intelligence may be highly heritable within a particular group of people living in a particular set of circumstances tells us nothing about whether or not differences between races are inherited.

It might appear that Rushton's theory is effectively demolished by the objections raised in the two paragraphs above. However, in order to be fair to Rushton we should inspect the evidence that he believes to provide support for it. This takes a number of forms.

First, he points out that widely differing species can be rated according to the extent to which their behaviour emphasizes high reproduction rates on the one hand or elevated levels of parental involvement on the other. For reasons that are not made at all clear he deduces that a similar kind of rating is viable when different groups of people within the human species are being compared. It hardly needs pointing out that from a biological perspective this is a somewhat breath-taking leap. It conveniently ignores the fact that all differences between human groups, including differences in genetic coding, are miniscule in comparison with inter-species variability.

Secondly, Rushton makes much of some findings that appear to demonstrate very small differences between brain sizes in people of different races. He introduces these results as evidence to support his theory despite the fact that, as he half-acknowledges, Stephen Jay Gould and others have demonstrated that accurate measures of human brain size are virtually impossible to obtain when one is restricted to the very crude methods of measurement available to the researchers whose work Rushton cites. That problem apart, for evidence about differences in brain sizes to have any real relevance to Rushton's theory it would need to have been shown that there is a cause-and-effect link between brain size and intelligence. This has not been satisfactorily established. In some investigations correlations of around .2 (accounting for less than a twentieth of the variability of individuals within a particular group) have been found, but in the absence of careful controlling for all the numerous other bodily dimensions that could be related to brain size (height, weight, length of various limbs, and so on) there is no justification for asserting that having larger brains than others causes people to be more intelligent. The fact that men have appreciably larger brains than women but are not more intelligent provides one indication of the implausibility of such a claim. Instances of geniuses with relatively small brains and case histories of individuals whose intelligence has remained following surgical removal of large parts of their brain provide further evidence contradicting Rushton.

Thirdly, and curiously, Rushton devotes four pages of his book to a discussion of the size of (mainly male) sexual organs. Rushton appears to believe that a large penis leads to a high procreation rate, although the reasons for his supposing this are never made at all clear, and no evidence is supplied to confirm that large penises do cause their possessors to produce more offspring than others. One might have expected that Rushton would at least have been careful to ensure that the measurement of penis size was accurate and reliable, but in fact all he did was to ask the individuals being assessed to make the size measurements themselves, using a piece of string, with no training or supervision. As with most of the research examining differences in brain size, little effort appears to have been made to take into account potentially covarying dimensions such as height and weight. The validity of the findings is further reduced by the fact that only a small minority of the individuals who participated in this study (who were paid out of Pioneer Fund income) acceded to the request for information on penis sizes, a request that some may have found more than a little puzzling. The participants could have been forgiven for believing that they had allowed themselves to become involved in an investigation on the wrong side of the line between science and pseudo-science. It is impossible to tell how carefully they complied with the instructions, or to what extent the information they supplied may have been influenced by subjective factors.

Fourthly, Rushton also collected evidence concerning various other aspects of sexual behaviour that he apparently believes to be indicative of high procreation rates. For instance, he requested information from 150 participants about age of first sexual intercourse and strength of semen emission (as indicated, in case you wish to know, by how far each male subject could ejaculate!). Rushton also asked both male and female participants about the frequency of multiple female orgasms.

(He discovered that the men in his study rated these as considerably more common than the women did.)

Race and IQ: The Evidence

Even though Rushton's evidence is hardly convincing and his theory is almost certainly wrong it remains conceivable that there are genetically caused differences in intelligence between racial groups. As we have seen, it is not easy to undertake research that directly investigates the question of whether or not such differences exist, but there are a number of research studies that have provided useful evidence concerning possible connections between racial ancestry and IQ.[1]

(1)   One study measured the IQs of several hundred German children who had been fathered in World War II by black GIs, and compared them with the IQs of children fathered by white GIs. If race and IQ were linked, we would expect to observe that the children fathered by white GIs would have had higher intelligence. In fact there were no differences, the averages being around 97 for both groups of children. This finding is clearly consistent with the view that there are no genetically caused differences in intelligence between different racial groups (Flynn, 1980).

(2)   Another investigation assessed the IQs of children amongst whom differences in the composition of their blood provided an indication of the varying extent to which individuals possessed 'European' and 'African' genes. Because of the fact that within the 'black' population of the United States there are differences between people in the extent to which they have European genes, it is possible to make some useful predictions. For instance, if genes are an important determinant of a person's IQ and there are racially linked genetic differences that affect intelligence, it would be expected that the larger the proportion of European as against African genes people possess, the higher their IQ. The study was carried out in Philadelphia, and the participants were a large sample of nearly 3,000 young black people. The main finding was that there was no statistically significant relationship at all between IQ and the genetic proportions estimated from the participants' blood composition (Scarr et al., 1977). So once again, the evidence clearly indicates

the absence of a relationship between degree of white ancestry and intellectual skills.

(3) Another study made a further search for a relationship between estimates of the European contribution to genetic composition, estimated from people's blood groups, and IQ scores. Two samples of black participants were tested. In one group the correlation between IQ and the European gene estimates was zero. In the other sample there was a correlation of .38, but in the 'wrong' direction. That is, individuals with characteristically African blood groups had higher rather than lower IQs than the other subjects (Loehlin et al., 1973).

(4) Adoption studies in which black children have been adopted by white parents have provided an additional source of evidence. The findings point to the conclusion that there are no genetically caused black–white differences in IQ. For instance, in an investigation by Scarr and Weinberg (1983) it was found that children whose biological parents were white and who were raised by white parents had slightly higher IQs than children with one black and one white biological parent and children with two black biological parents. The small differences in IQ scores were entirely in line with what would have been expected as a result of various influences that favoured the white children, such as variations in prenatal environments, selective placement of adopted children, problems caused by being the only black member of a white family, differences in rearing practices prior to adoption, and the kinds of black–white differences in experiences associated with discrimination and with adults' lower expectations of academic success in black compared with white children.

Another study compared the intelligence of children with black (Caribbean) and white biological parents who were reared together in a residential institution (Tizard et al., 1972). Their IQs at the age of four averaged 103 for the white children, 106 for the children of mixed race, and 108 for the children whose biological parents were both black. So once again, there was absolutely no evidence for the white children being genetically superior.

Interestingly, Rushton mentions the fact that adopted white children have been found to have slightly higher IQs than adopted black children, and he insists on urging hereditarian explanations of the group differences even when there is compelling evidence of substantial variability in individuals' experiences. For example, where the authors of one study attributed the poorer performance of black adopted children to their experience of more difficult circumstances of adoption and lower educational levels of the natural and the adoptive parents, Rushton asserts, without giving a reason, that the real reason for the difference was that blacks have lower mental ability than whites because of their African ancestry. Facts can be ignored, it appears, when they contradict Rushton's beliefs. Similarly, Rushton insists that findings showing that the likelihood of criminal behaviour in adopted children is slightly more highly correlated with criminality in biological than adopted parents proves that inherited determinants are all-important. He appears to be unaware of the fact that adoptees from criminal backgrounds have often had particularly disturbed childhoods.

(5) In one investigation, in which the participants were highly intelligent black children, information about their family backgrounds was used to classify the children according to the degree to which their ancestry had a European (white) element. Contrary to what would be expected if it was true that racial differences in genetic composition have effects on intelligence that favour white individuals, the participating children were found to have less rather than more European ancestry on average than the black American population as a whole. This finding provides yet more evidence that is inconsistent with the view that genetic differences between races are a major influence on intelligence (Witty and Jenkins, 1934).

(6) If genetic racial composition is a major cause of differences, in intelligence, children who have a black mother and white father would have the same or similar average IQs as children with white mothers and black fathers. However, if differences between black and white children in their average IQs are largely the result of socialization and learning experiences, with white mothers providing more early stimulation, a different outcome would be expected. Because most children spend more time with their mother than with their father, the children with a white mother and a black father would have higher IQs on average than the children with a black mother and a white father.

In a research investigation, precisely that was observed. The IQs of children from mixed unions were nine points higher, on average, when it was the mother who was white. Interestingly, that finding was obtained despite the fact that a higher proportion of the white mothers were unmarried. Because being an unmarried mother is an indication of low IQ (in sample averages, rather than in individuals), one would have expected that if genetic influences were important those children born to the white mothers would have had lower IQs than the others. The fact that this was not the case at all, and that these children had considerably higher rather than lower IQ scores, strongly points to the conclusion that differences in early experiences, perhaps resulting from contrasting parenting practices, are the primary cause of any racial differences in the IQ scores.

Conclusion

Taking all the findings together, they strongly point to the conclusion that there are no genetic differences in intelligence favouring white children. The results of a substantial number of research studies have failed to produce any evidence of such differences. Not only is Rushton's theory of racial differences wrong, but the assertion by 'racial scientists' that there exist inherent differences in intelligence related to racial background is totally mistaken.

The one verifiable difference that needs explaining is in average IQ scores. A number of investigations have estimated that in the United States whites surpass blacks by around 10 IQ points. There is evidence that this difference is diminishing, and from the statistics collected by James Flynn (see Chapter 3), showing considerable increases in intelligence scores from one decade to the next as the health and economic and educational circumstances of people improve, it appears likely that the difference may be wiped out in a generation or so. Moreover, some of the observed differences in scores between racial groups contradict rather than match the predictions of Rushton's racial theory. For example, the average scores of Native Americans, which according to Rushton ought to be somewhat higher than those of the white population, are in fact appreciably lower.

Despite the marked absence of evidence genuinely supporting their views, race theorists seem to believe that the sheer fact that there are differences in test scores is sufficient justification for deducing that genetic causes are involved. In fact, however, the causes almost certainly lie in the different life experiences of black and white individuals. But for Rushton and others who believe that racial differences in achievements have genetic origins, the possibility that differences in culture and experience are the real causes of the black–white difference in IQ scores is believed to be ruled out because a small difference between black and white children remains even when the number of years of schooling and the economic status of the parents are equivalent.

That line of reasoning depends upon the assumption that controlling just these factors eliminates all the potentially influential differences between children in the culture to which they are exposed and in their early experiences. It takes only a moment's reflection to perceive how wrong that assumption is. It is well known that the educational environments provided by ghetto schools and the schools attended by the children of highly educated parents who live in prosperous areas are vastly different, and that the home and family circumstances of those who attend them vary even more. The kinds of family experiences that can be made available by parents who are highly educated, articulate, and self-confident, and whose family circumstances are buttressed by generations of wealth and success, who give their children plenty of support and encouragement and provide them with plenty of learning opportunities and matching expectations, cannot easily be matched by families who have experienced generations of oppression and poverty. Slavery, discrimination, and the accompanying injustices have had consequences that are not easily reversed. The effects of racism, as the writer John Sedgwick has remarked 'like the bloodstains on the hands of Lady Macbeth, cannot be washed away' (1995: 158).

There are numerous ways in which the differences in children's early circumstances equip them differently for succeeding at the kinds of problems encountered by a child who is given an intelligence test. Just one of the many causes of major differences in children's learning experiences is demonstrated in the investigation by Betty Hart and Todd Risley (1995), previously mentioned in Chapter 3. It was shown that there are differences in the order of millions in the number of opportunities children brought up in differing family backgrounds have to experience language that is directed towards them. Over many generations black citizens have been far more likely than whites to grow up poor, fatherless, malnourished, badly educated, unemployed, living in substandard accommodation in neglected urban environments, victimized by crime and drugs. Keeping people powerless makes them passive and fatalistic, lacking confidence in their capacity to succeed in a world where others pull the strings. Depriving minorities of opportunities and encouragement helps keep them deskilled and ignorant. For better or worse, it is simply not true that all the negative cultural influences are removed at a stroke as soon as a few people from disadvantaged minorities gain a modicum of prosperity and some reasonably adequate schooling, perhaps augmented by a summer or two in a Head Start programme.

Note

1. This section draws upon a valuable discussion of the issue by Nisbett (1995).

5

Is High IQ a Necessity?

Is it essential to have a high IQ in order to do well at mental tasks and solve difficult problems? If the answer to the question is sometimes 'No', that would suggest that the qualities assessed in an IQ test may not play so vital a role in a person's intellectual capacities as is usually assumed. It would also make another dent in the belief that the IQ scores tap crucial inherent qualities underlying an individual's mental capabilities.

People with high IQs do tend to do well at a variety of tasks demanding mental competence. But it does not necessarily follow that they do well *because* of their high IQs. Even if IQ tests simply sample a person's acquired abilities, we would expect there to be a positive relationship between IQ scores and performance at other tasks, so long as there is a reasonably good match between the abilities assessed in IQ tests and the mental skills and knowledge required in order to act intelligently in the real world. After all, even if IQ tests do more than sample someone's knowledge and skills, IQ scores ought to be reasonable guides to the level of a person's mental functioning. But in that case we would also expect that people with low IQs will sometimes do well at difficult mental tasks, and people with high IQs will sometimes do poorly.

However, much firmer predictions would be possible if the capacities that determine someone's IQ level are more than just a sample of abilities, and do reflect some inherent quality of the person, distinct from and more fundamental than the person's other capabilities. In that event, having a low IQ would point to definite limitations in a person's cognitive capacities. A consequence would be that someone with a low IQ would be simply incapable of certain mental feats. And in that case, because a low IQ indicated the absence of essential basic capacities, it would be entirely realistic to say that a person failed to solve a problem because he or she had too low an IQ.

So, contrasting predictions are generated by the two differing views about the meaning of a person's IQ score. If IQ scores simply reflect the products of acquired abilities, we would expect to find an imperfect match between someone's scores and his or her other achievements. But if a person's IQ score reflects fundamental attributes that mental accomplishments depend upon, certain tasks would be simply impossible for someone with a low IQ. We can shed light on the question of which of the two contrasting views is the correct one by discovering whether or not it is actually true that low IQs rule out success at difficult mental problems.

Complex Reasoning in Low-IQ Individuals

Various sources of information have contributed useful evidence. Consider first some research findings that were obtained in the unlikely setting of a horse-racing track (Ceci and Liker, 1986). The participants in the study were gamblers who attended hundreds of (harness) race meetings every year. Unsurprisingly, they had all become very knowledgeable about racing. In addition, some of these racetrack gamblers had become capable of undertaking some complex and elaborate mental calculations that can be helpful to someone who bets on horse races, by making it possible to estimate a horse's form and predict the likely race odds. This gives a gambler an edge, enabling the identification of any horse that has a better chance of winning than the actual track odds suggest.

In order to carry out the necessary mental calculations it is necessary for the gambler to take into account various kinds of data that have a bearing on a horse's current form. These include information about the condition of the racecourse and detailed data relating to past performances, including previous times and race positions and other factors such as the extent to which a horse consumed its energy in bursts of speed or overtaking, and its position on the racecourse in relation to the rails. The aim is to arrive at an estimate of a horse's real speed and strength after making allowances for all the other influences that might have affected past performances. What makes the task especially complicated is that it is not just a matter of summing together the combined influences, because they interact with one another, in complicated, non-additive ways.

The researchers, Stephen Ceci and Jeffrey Liker, set the gamblers (all of whom were men) a series of difficult mental calculation tasks that involved estimating the future odds on horses on the basis of various items of information about recent race performances. Despite the fact that it is impossible to do well at these handicapping or odds-setting problems without being capable of highly complex kinds of reasoning, a substantial proportion of the racetrack gamblers had a high measure of success.

Ceci and Liker then examined the relationship between a person's expertise at this task and the same individual's IQ. Since success at these problems depended on the gambler being able to carry out mental operations of considerable complexity, it might have been expected that there would be a strong positive relationship between gamblers' success at the task and their IQ levels. It would also appear likely that low-IQ individuals would be incapable of doing well. In fact, the results contradicted both these expectations. That is, the correlation (or relationship) between someone's level of success and his IQ was zero, and some of those men who were most successful at mastering the problems had below-average IQs. In contrast, some of the individuals who, despite their keen interest in horse racing, had not gained the expertise that enabled them to solve the problems set by the researchers, were well-educated high-IQ individuals with university degrees and professional qualifications.

These results are hard to reconcile with the viewpoint that the level of a person's IQ score points to the presence or absence of fundamental intellectual capacities. The finding that certain individuals with low IQs are capable of complex cognitive processing seems to contradict the belief that the capacities that are assessed in an IQ test are all-important.

Is it possible that racetrack gamblers form some kind of unique anomaly? Could they be a rare and untypical breed of individuals who happen to be good at complex problems but poor at taking intelligence tests? That possibility appears to be ruled out by the fact that other investigations have identified

additional situations in which people's expertise at intellectually demanding tasks is unrelated to their general intelligence level. In one such investigation (Scribner, 1984)
researchers observed the workers in a dairy. Their job was to fill
orders for differing amounts of various products. This involved
a fair amount of bending and lifting, and many of the workers
had devised sophisticated strategies for working efficiently
by reducing this to a minimum, wasting as little energy as
possible.

To help understand what was involved in the dairy workers'
tasks, imagine that you are working in a dairy yourself. You are
told to fill an order for 6 pints of whole milk, 12 pints of 2 per
cent milk, and 3 pints each of skim milk and buttermilk.
Around you there are a number of partly filled boxes of these
products. In order to be an efficient worker and avoid wasting
energy you have to decide how to get the job done with the least
amount of heavy lifting.

Let's assume that there is a 24-pint case that is already half-
filled with 2 per cent milk and one-third filled with whole milk.
Would it be sensible to start with that one, or would it be easier
to choose another partly filled case containing different combinations of milk? Or might it be better to begin with an
entirely empty case? Making the most effective decisions in this
situation demands some fairly complicated mental operations,
involving arithmetical reasoning processes that are very similar
to the ones required for using different number bases in formal
mathematics. To find the most efficient way to fill each order it
is necessary to have an implicit understanding of different
number bases.

Evidently, the dairy workers studied in this investigation,
like the racetrack gamblers in the previous one, had to be
capable of complex mental functioning. It was therefore important to know something about those employees who consistently
succeeded in arriving at solutions that involved the least
amount of moving and lifting. In particular, was their success at
doing this related to their IQ scores? The researchers discovered
that it was not: the extent to which individuals reached the best
solutions was unrelated to either their IQ scores or their level of
education.

In yet another investigation, a German research team headed
by D. Dörner (cited in Ceci, 1990) asked people to imagine that

they were in charge of a small city. It had the competing needs and problems of real cities, including inflation, unemployment, and the necessity to raise revenues for roads and other services. Making effective managerial decisions demanded mental flexibility and complex thinking, and taking into account a number of interacting and sometimes conflicting considerations. For example, it was necessary to produce revenues, using mechanisms that did not have seriously adverse effects on interest rates, but it was also important to avoid making municipal bonds unattractive to investors, since that could have various negative outcomes. Once again, as in the racetrack and dairy studies, the investigators were interested in discovering to what, if any, extent the ability of individual participants to do well at this intellectually demanding task was related to their formal education and intelligence. Once more, there was found to be no relationship at all.

In short, none of these three studies provides any support at all for the position that a person's ability to engage in complex mental functioning depends at all closely upon that person's IQ. Taken together, these findings add to the case made in the previous chapter for the view that the capabilities that determine a person's IQ scores do *not* take the form of inherent fundamental capacities that underly other mental skills.

A possible objection is that investigations such as the three I have described form a somewhat piecemeal selection of studies. The fact that a few situations can be located in which IQ and alternative indications of a person's intelligence level are unrelated does not rule out the possibility that these are positively related in the vast majority of circumstances. However, an additional source of evidence, involving individuals with unusual patterns of capabilities and handicaps, has yielded a more substantial body of relevant findings.

Unusual Patterns of Ability

A number of investigators have looked at the unusual patterns of ability and disability that are presented by certain individuals who are mentally handicapped, having very low IQs, but who are nevertheless capable of exceptionally high levels of performance within particular domains of mental ability. These

people, some of whom are also autistic and have restricted
social awareness, are usually known as 'idiots savants' or
simply 'savants'.

Numerous cases of exceptional feats by mentally handicapped
savants have been reported. The accomplishments can take any
of a number of forms, including musical or artistic ones, unusual language skills, various remarkable feats of memory, and
exceptional calculating based on mental arithmetic. An attain-
ment that is described in a large proportion of the published
reports of savants' skills involves being able to state the correct
day of the week on which any specified calendar date falls. This
skill, known as 'calendar calculating', has a number of components, and in most cases partly depends upon the person
having memorized considerable amounts of information about
calendars.

How can savants be capable of skills that draw upon a
substantial number of the mental capacities that are normally
associated with high intelligence, despite having IQs that are
well below average and sometimes as low as 50 or less? It is
hard to explain their unusual juxtapositions of expertise and
retardation. It is especially difficult to see how an approach that
insists that IQ levels give an indication of the extent to which
different individuals possess basic cognitive capacities that
intellectual abilities draw upon could account for these
mentally handicapped savants, with their islands of ability in
the form of fragmentary skills standing out from a person's
highly restricted mental functioning in other areas. Although
some efforts have been made to reconcile the achievements of
savants with intelligence theory, which insists that there exists
some general quality of intelligence underlying particular
attainments, these have been less than successful. The
attempts revolve around the unlikely assumption that the
brains of savants differ in fundamental ways from those of
ordinary people. In my view it is more likely that the sharply
contrasting abilities and disabilities of savants are simply extreme manifestations of the irregular profiles of ability present
in many 'normal' people.

That suggestion is also consistent with the finding that even
in people of normal intelligence the capacity to solve problems
may vary enormously from one situation to another. The variability in a single person's level of performance at apparently

similar tasks can be large, providing grounds for questioning the assumption that people have fixed specific abilities, let alone a fixed general intelligence. For instance, in one investigation, which took place in Liberia, the researchers asked some students and some men who were employed as skilled tailors to attempt arithmetical questions (Lave, 1977). Each question could be presented either as a tailoring problem (involving measurements used in working with cloth) or in the form of a typical school task. Even when the formal arithmetic needed in order to solve a problem was identical, the tailors did far better if it was posed in a tailoring context than if it was presented as a school task. The best predictor of success was the person's number of years experience as a tailor. But the reverse applied when the identical arithmetical task was presented as a school-type problem, with no tailoring context. When the arithmetical problems were presented as school tasks, the best predictor of a person's success was the number of years of schooling the individual had received.

Context and Problem Solving

Further evidence that people's mental skills may be fluid rather than fixed comes from some research conducted in Brazil, where researchers studied children who make a living by selling lottery tickets (Schliemann, 1988). In order to do well at their job, some of these children have developed a sophisticated understanding of mathematical probabilities. But if they are given school-type problems designed to test exactly the same probability skills they employ so effectively for dealing in tickets, they cannot solve them at all. Conversely, students who have learned about probability in school lessons do far worse than the street children when given tasks in which they have to apply the rules learned at school in out-of-school contexts. So once again, even when problems are formally identical, an individual's capacity to solve them greatly depends upon the particular context in which they are presented.

In another investigation researchers examined children's ability to estimate the movements of small shapes on a video screen (Ceci, 1990). Once more, in each of two conditions the problem was formally identical, and the only difference was in the manner in which the task was portrayed. In the first condition, children were told to look at various objects shown on the screens and had to try to predict where each object would move to next. They did this by moving a cross that appeared on the screen, using a joystick. Each screen object could be one of three different shapes, two colours, and two sizes, making 12 possible combinations of object features. Objects' movements were determined by various rules, such as squares go up, circles go down, dark objects move right, light objects move left, large objects move in one direction, and small objects in the opposite direction. Over a large number of trials, the children tried to learn these rules governing the movements of the objects, and use this knowledge to make accurate predictions. However, they totally failed to do so: even after 15 50-trial sessions at the task most participants were only performing at around chance level.

In the other condition the participants were given essentially the same problem, but the way in which it was explained to them was different. These children were informed that they were playing a video game. The items they saw on the screen were the same colours and sizes, and their movements were governed by the same rules, but the objects were changed from being squares, circles, and triangles to butterflies, bumblebees, and birds. And rather than just being told to put a cross at the place on the screen where they thought the object would move to, they were asked to try to 'capture the prey'. They did this by moving the joystick (just as in the other condition), but they, unlike the others, were told that by doing that they were moving a 'butterfly net' to the location they decided upon.

These changes in the way in which the task was explained to the participants had a huge effect on performance. Children in the second condition did far better than the others, getting near-perfect scores. Once again, the individuals' performance levels were greatly affected by the differing contexts, and once more, the findings challenge the assumption that a person's abilities can be regarded as fixed qualities.

The observation that people's capabilities at various mental problems are greatly affected by the contexts in which problems are presented does nothing to increase confidence in the idea that a person's intelligence level can be represented by a single score. Neither does the fact that it is not difficult to find examples of impressive abilities in people with low IQs. These results seem to contradict the belief that a low IQ indicates that essential capacities that underly intelligent functioning must be absent. They also raise the possibility that specific human capabilities are more separate from one another, and more independent and autonomous, than they are usually thought to be, and fluid rather than fixed. Confirming this would strike a further blow at intelligence theory and the psychometric approach to intelligence, by suggesting that the general level of a person's intelligence exerts few if any constraints upon what a person is actually capable of doing.

Because we are so used to thinking that how well people do at tasks that are intellectually demanding depends upon how intelligent they are, we often take it for granted that knowing a person's level of intelligence helps to *explain* his or her strengths and limitations. But as I mentioned earlier, in Chapter 2, that assumption may be quite wrong. In fact, there are strong grounds for arguing that specifying a person's intelligence level only *describes* what he or she does, and cannot explain anything. The reasons are much the same as the ones that are responsible for the fact that having high productivity does not explain why a factory produces large amounts of goods.

There are yet more reasons for believing that a person's different skills are to a considerable extent fragmentary, in the sense of being independent of one another and unconstrained by the individual's level of intelligence. First, numerous findings from research into the effects of brain damage have demonstrated that particular abilities of a person may be totally destroyed whilst others, even very similar ones, stay unimpaired. Secondly, a number of studies have shown that ordinary people can gain specific mental skills that are quite exceptional, but that when this happens the person's other abilities are unaffected. For instance, as was mentioned in the previous chapter, prolonged training can produce vast increases in people's memory spans for digits, but the training has virtually no effect on the individuals' memories for lists containing other kinds of information such as letters or words. Finally, there are studies demonstrating that contrary to what would be expected if apparently similar abilities are closely interdependent or interlocked, activities that impede performance at one task may have little or no effect upon another similar one. A person may even be able to perform two highly similar tasks at the same time. These results suggest that even when similar or apparently related abilities are involved, the mental mechanisms that make them possible may be to a surprising extent distinct.

Why are Abilities Correlated?

Although the findings outlined in the present chapter strongly point to the conclusion that a person's specific cognitive abilities are largely independent of IQ, it is nevertheless true that there are correlations between people's performance levels at various abilities. That is, people who do well at one kind of mental task or problem tend to do well at another cognitive task. Equally, someone who achieves a certain level of performance at one of the sub-tests in an IQ test will tend to have a similar level of performance at other sub-tests. The fact that there are these correlations is one of the reasons for the widespread, if erroneous, belief that IQ scores reflect underlying mental capacities. So it needs to be asked, if that view is misguided, why is it that we do find positive correlations between people's abilities. What other explanation can there be?

As it happens, it is not at all difficult to think of alternative reasons for people's different mental abilities being correlated, without assuming that specific abilities depend either on IQ level or on some other kind of general intelligence. One possible explanation is that whenever a person's performance at two mental tasks is assessed, the chances are that each task will draw upon a number of specific skills and elements of knowledge, and it is often the case that one or more of these will be shared between the two tasks. That is, one of any two problems may contain elements that are shared with the other task. So a reason for measures of a person's performance at two problems being correlated is that each problem draws upon mental capacities that have elements in common.

A second reason is that even when there are no common elements in the two tasks, there may be characteristics of the person attempting them that have similar effects on performance at both. There are numerous personal attributes that are likely to exert similar effects on the likelihood of someone succeeding at each of a number of problems, even very different ones. Some of these attributes may be related to a person's temperament, character, or personality, or may reflect the individual's interests, lifestyle, mood, attitude to life, or established habits. The many attributes of a person that would lead to someone tending to have similar levels of success at unrelated tasks include self-confidence, competitiveness, attentiveness, willingness to persevere, fatigue, capacity to concentrate, degree of interest, degree of personal involvement, patience, 'test-wiseness', cooperativeness, assertiveness, optimism, level of motivation, and ability to resist distractions. If any of these exert similar influences on a person's performance at each of a number of problems, the result will be that performance levels at the different tasks will be correlated. If, in addition, there are common elements in each of a pair of tasks, the correlations will be augmented.

With any pair of cognitive tasks or problems such as the ones that are encountered in IQ tests there is a reasonable probability either that there are elements common to both, or that there are attributes of the person taking the test that will similarly affect performance at each. Quite often, both of these conditions will be present. Consequently, the fact that there are similarities in a person's levels of performance at different tasks should be no occasion for surprise. It is certainly no justification for believing in the existence of some governing quality of intelligence or an underlying general mental ability; there are simpler ways of accounting for the correlations.

The Implications of Intelligence Levels

What does it mean to have a high IQ, or a low IQ? What does knowing someone's IQ score tell us about the person? A person's score undoubtedly tells us how well that individual has performed at a test made up of items that tap a variety of cognitive skills and items of knowledge that are broadly similar to mental abilities that receive attention in the school curriculum. Consequently, an IQ score is a reasonable guide to someone's ability to solve problems that require the kinds of intelligence that are related to school learning. But is a score more than that? The research findings reported in the present chapter and the previous one suggest not. An IQ level does not point to inherent or immutable qualities of the person. It does not demonstrate the existence of mental capacities that are fundamental to other mental skills, or underly acquired abilities. Nor does it identify constraints that limit what someone is capable of learning.

Essentially, a person's IQ is no more than an indication of how someone performed at a series of mental tasks. As I suggested in Chapter 2, that kind of knowledge does not explain anything. Knowing someone's IQ does not establish *why* that person acts intelligently, just as knowing that a car is fast does not explain why it is capable of moving speedily, and knowing that one factory is unusually productive does not help us to understand why it makes more goods than another.

There is a common error of thinking, whereby people start to believe that if a word exists it must refer to some identifiable concrete thing. So, because the term 'intelligence' is in widespread use to refer to the quality of being intelligent, there is the tendency to 'reify' that concept mentioned in Chapter 2, and assume that intelligence must be some 'thing' that people possess to varying degrees, and which causes people to be intelligent. The obvious implication is that people are intelligent because they have intelligence.

It is very easy to fall into this way of thinking, which coincides with many people's commonsense beliefs, and the fact that it is likely to be fallacious only becomes obvious when other familiar concepts are submitted to the same treatment (Howe, 1990b). For example, people who are successful are said to have success, but we can readily perceive the error of deducing that someone is successful *because* of their success, just as we immediately see that an automobile is not fast because of its speed. In each case, despite appearances, the abstract noun does not actually refer to any underlying quality that can explain why events occur.

But in the case of intelligence matters are a little more complicated. Although what has been said about how easy it is to mistakenly reify terms demonstrates that this *may* have occurred with the concept of intelligence, so that, in common with 'success' or 'productivity', measured intelligence cannot genuinely explain anything (let alone itself), that is not an inevitable state of affairs. It is not inconceivable that intelligence really is a genuinely explanatory concept, after all. For instance, were it to turn out that a person's score in an intelligence test was not just an indication of performance at the test but also provided information about the presence or absence of qualities that contributed to the person's level of performance, there would be grounds for saying that an intelligence measure such as IQ can be genuinely explanatory. For that reason it has been necessary to examine evidence that would help decide if that was indeed the case. However, having examined the evidence, we are now in a position to see that there are no obvious grounds for regarding the intelligence that is reflected in an IQ score as being an explanatory concept. Knowing a person's IQ tells us nothing that helps explain why he or she succeeds or fails.

Can we be sure that this conclusion is correct? Is it really true that establishing that a person has a high IQ does nothing all to help explain why that individual does well at various tasks and problems, except in the trivial sense of saying that someone with a high IQ performs well because he or she 'has what it takes' to do so? Isn't it possible that by specifying a person's IQ level we are also providing evidence about whether that person is, say, good at learning, or has an efficient memory, or has a capacity for abstract reasoning? In other words, could it be that despite the apparent complete lack of empirical support for the idea that measured intelligence is an explanatory concept, knowing about someone's IQ nevertheless does something to help to explain why that person is capable or incapable of reaching certain levels of achievement?

In order to investigate this possibility I considered a number of the attributes that are commonly thought to be implied by high intelligence (Howe, 1988, 1989a). For example, there is a frequently stated view that someone who is intelligent must be good at learning. Another common belief is that an intelligent person must have a good memory. A third view is that an intelligent individual, unlike an unintelligent one, is capable of abstract reasoning. Another is that differences in level of intelligence indicate clear differences between people in their capacity to think or reason logically. Other possibilities are that differences in measured intelligence reflect individuals' varying degrees of flexibility in their capacity to utilize their mental skills, or adapt existing skills to the demands of new or unfamiliar situations. Also, differences in intelligence are sometimes thought to indicate varying ability to plan and coordinate a person's mental resources.

Almost certainly, all of these capacities are correlated with intelligence. That is, it is true that intelligent people tend to be successful learners, good at remembering, effective planners, and so on. But in order to show that by saying someone is intelligent something is really being explained, for example by identifying the person as being a good learner or a logical thinker or a clever planner, it is necessary to established that these attributes are directly linked to intelligence level. Otherwise the observed relationships between IQ level and the capacity to perform those functions can be accounted for by observing that high IQ levels merely point to the likelihood of a person possessing certain acquired knowledge and skills that the above challenges necessitate. For instance, it could be claimed that the reason why intelligent people tend to be logical thinkers is simply that the kinds of acquired knowledge and skills that help a person to score well in an intelligence test also help a person to think logically. So although there may be a correlation, there is not necessarily any non-trivial or causal connection; there may not be any necessity to have a high IQ in order to succeed at the thinking problems. The important questions remain unanswered. Does an indication of someone's intelligence level tell us anything directly about his or her actual capacity to think, or remember, or learn, as such?

Perhaps surprisingly, the answers appear to be negative. With learning, for instance, it has proved impossible to provide evidence of connections between learning and measured intelligence other than those that can be explained as being a consequence of acquired knowledge and skills. As it happens, finding an indication of a person's basic capacity to learn that is not contaminated by previous learning and experiences is not at all easy. The kinds of learning situation that best approximate that are very simple ones. They involve forms of 'conditioning' in which two events, when presented together on a number of occasions, come to be perceived as linked. For example, if a light is briefly shone and a puff of air to the eye are delivered together on a number of occasions, eventually the blink that occurs as a response to the puff of air also occurs when the light is shone even when the puff is absent, demonstrating that the individual's mind has made some kind of link between the two kinds of events. When people's performance in situations involving this kind of learning is assessed, it is found to be unrelated to intelligence level. In fact it has also been discovered that young children and mentally retarded individuals tend to do just as well as adults (Estes, 1970). That finding provides no support at all for the idea that each person has a basic capacity to learn that is directly connected to his or her intelligence.

Similarly, there appears to be no direct connection between IQ levels and remembering. In those memory tasks in which there is little scope for performance to be improved by adopting acquired strategies or making use of previously gained knowledge, it has been discovered that young children typically perform just as well as adults do. It may not even be true that there exists a unitary memory ability at all, let alone one that is closely dependent upon intelligence. The former belief is called into question by the finding that when people are asked to perform a number of different memory tasks, correlations between level of performance at the different tasks are generally very low (Howe, 1989a).

With each of the other mental processes, evidence of direct links to measured intelligence is similarly lacking. In the case of reasoning, for example, whilst it is certainly true that intelligent people tend to be better thinkers than unintelligent people, that is probably because performance at reasoning tasks is strongly affected by people's familiarity with the task contents and their knowledge of the circumstances. With abstract thinking, too, there appears to be no direct link to IQ level. Investigating that matter is made difficult by the fact that it is hard to agree on a way of rating tasks for degree of abstractness, but it is clear that even some mentally retarded savants, with very low IQs and limited comprehension, are quite capable of abstract thought in connection with certain kinds of problem (Howe, 1989b).

So far as a possible link between intelligence and flexibility is concerned, it is hard to locate firm evidence, but once again some research findings point to the absence of a direct connection. For example, it has been found that the effectiveness of adjustment to military life by men with mild mental handicap is unrelated to intelligence. Also, correlations between childhood

IQ scores and ratings of success at everyday tasks of adult life are very low, accounting for less than 5 per cent of the variability in performance (Howe, 1989a).

In short, there appears to be little evidence that firm statements about what a person is actually capable of achieving can be firmly deduced from knowing an individual's IQ level. That is not to deny that someone with a given level of IQ is more likely to succeed than someone with a lower IQ at solving problems that depend on mental skills and knowledge, and that information may be very useful; for instance it may enable predictions to be made about the likelihood of the person being able to deal with various real-life situations that require mental skills. But IQs are not at all informative concerning the reasons *why* people differ. They cannot help us to understand why one person is more intelligent than another.

Conclusion: Is it Possible to be a Genius with a Low IQ?

In this chapter I have provided numerous illustrations of people whose IQs are low but who are nevertheless capable of impressive intellectual feats. Are there any limits to this? Is it conceivable, for example, that someone could be a genius and yet have a low IQ?

Strangely enough, that may not be impossible. Take the case of the great railway engineer George Stephenson, whose face appears on every English five pound note. Stephenson, who was born in 1781, was a remarkably inventive genius whose many achievements led to the first practical application of passenger steam locomotion when the Liverpool to Manchester line was opened in 1830. And yet Stephenson never went to school as a child and could not even write his name or do any but the simplest arithmetic before he was 18; nor did he ever really master written English. He was undoubtedly intelligent, but had intelligence tests been available at the time, his illiteracy and innumeracy, coupled with a practical man's lack of interest in abstract problems, would almost certainly have resulted in a low IQ test score.

6

Using IQ Scores to Make Predictions

This chapter raises some straightforward questions about the practical applications of intelligence tests. It inquires into the extent to which IQ scores are useful for making predictions about people and their abilities. Often, waste and inefficiency can be avoided by making sure that people who are appointed to jobs are intelligent enough to do them properly, or by ensuring that individuals who are accepted for an educational programme possess the mental skills that will allow them to succeed. Do intelligence tests help achieve those aims?

The extent to which a test is effective depends partly on what it is being used for. Intelligence test scores are fairly good predictors of a child's progress at school, and on the whole tests are useful for predicting adult performance at problems that are similar to school tasks. But even the strongest supporters of intelligence testing concede that it is no magic wand. Howard Gardner (1995) has pointed out that almost all of the reported correlations between test scores and the educational, vocational, and other social outcomes they might be expected to predict account for no more than 20 per cent of the variability between people. That means that at least 80 per cent, and perhaps much more, of the contributing influences lie outside whatever is assessed by giving someone an intelligence test. Moreover, IQ scores may fail to provide good measures of the everyday intelligence of whole groups of people, let alone individuals. That is demonstrated by the findings of research undertaken by James Flynn (1991), investigating the abilities of Chinese immigrants to the United States.

Flynn looked at data on Chinese people who had immigrated to America after World War II. Their IQs were below the average for whites, and yet the real-life achievements of these

Chinese immigrants easily exceeded the achievements of individuals born in the United States. For example, among the immigrants over 50 per cent gained professional occupational status, which is almost twice the comparable proportion among white Americans. There are a number of possible reasons for this, including a willingness on the part of Chinese individuals to work hard for long hours. But whatever the explanation, these findings show that it cannot be taken for granted that IQ scores will always be good indicators of a person's level of achievement.

Generally speaking, IQ scores do generate predictions that are better than random guesses. They provide information about people's capacities to achieve practical kinds of success such as doing well at demanding jobs. However, there is considerable disagreement about the reasons why IQ scores predict. Perhaps that is because they provide good indicators of the mental skills and knowledge a person has acquired, or perhaps the fact that scores aid selection is simply a by-product of the fact that getting certain jobs requires educational credentials that are reflected in IQ scores. In that event IQ scores could be predictors for the rather trivial reason that they reflect success at overcoming some educational hurdle that is used to restrict entry to a job or profession. Alternatively, it is possible that scores yield predictions because, as intelligence theorists believe, they are genuine measures of some underlying quality – such as Spearman's g – that provides the energy for fuelling mental accomplishments.

How good are the predictions? That varies considerably from one set of circumstances to another. Moreover, different experts have varying opinions about the extent to which intelligence tests aid in the making of accurate predictions.

IQs as Predictors: The Positive Claims

The authors of *The Bell Curve* take a favourable view of testing, although even they concede that the correlations between IQ and indicators of, say, occupational success are modest, generally between .2 and .6. Correlations of this magnitude account for 36 per cent of the variability between people at the very best, and only 4 per cent at worst. These authors suggest that, on average, correlations between IQ and measures of job performance are around .4 (Herrnstein and Murray, 1994: 72). That figure implies a 16 per cent contribution to individual variability, close to Gardner's estimate of 20 per cent. The correlations tend to be slightly higher than this for skilled and managerial jobs and slightly lower for jobs that require less skill. Estimates of *g* have also been found to be relatively good predictors of performance at certain specific jobs within the armed services (Herrnstein and Murray, 1994: 76).

The practical implications of these figures depend on whether one wishes to make predictions about individuals as such or only about the average success of large groups of people. So far as an individual person is concerned, knowing that person's test score is likely to improve predictions only to a very limited extent, if at all. It might not be worth going to the trouble of administering an intelligence test, especially if the time that would take could be used for gaining other useful information about the person's capabilities.

The implications are different, however, if the aim is to make predictions about a large number of people. Imagine that a large company wishes to appoint a hundred new employees to jobs demanding a certain level of mental ability. There are a thousand applicants, and the company knows nothing about their capacities. In this case, selecting people on the basis of the IQ scores would be more efficient than choosing them at random. Wastage would be avoided, thereby reducing unnecessary expenditure for the company.

The Bell Curve provides an illustration of the value of testing for personnel selection when large numbers are involved (Herrnstein and Murray, 1994: 87). In 1939 the New York City police force advertised for 300 positions, attracting no less than 30,000 applicants. It was decided to allocate the jobs largely on the basis of performance at a written test that was similar in content to an intelligence test then in use, and the positions were accordingly filled by the top scorers. These individuals turned out to be an excellent set of policemen, with less disciplinary problems than would be expected in an average entry of that size. Many of the group had successful careers, a dozen of them reaching very senior positions in the police service.

IQs as Predictors: Critical Views

Other psychologists have taken a less favourable view of the practical value of testing. Some researchers have argued that the true average correlations between intelligence and job performance may be nearer .2 than .4. In that event they could account for less than half a per cent of individual variation (McClelland, 1973). In one investigation it was discovered that adjustment to military life was unrelated to intelligence test scores (Zigler and Seitz, 1982). In another study the researchers, who observed senior managers actually performing their jobs, concluded that the mental abilities necessary for succeeding as a manager are very different from the skills assessed in IQ tests (Klemp and McClelland, 1986). Also, as was noted in Chapter 5, there have been a number of demonstrations that individuals' performance at job-related tasks may be completely unrelated to their intelligence test scores.

Another critical point is that even when there exist modest correlations between IQ and job success, the positive relationship may be restricted to people's early months in the job. Leon Kamin (1995) drew attention to the fact that in a number of studies it has been shown that the relationships between performance and IQ reduce to zero by the time workers have been doing the job for several years. In some cases, after four or five years of experience low-IQ workers were actually outperforming co-workers with higher IQ scores.

IQs and Other Predictors

Investigators have drawn attention to the fact that even when test scores are modestly good predictors of various practical outcomes, that need not mean that high IQ is necessary for real-life success: it can simply be a side-effect of IQ scores being correlated with more important influences. Consider, for instance, the correlations between men's childhood IQs and their economic success as adults. These are moderately high, as much as around .8 in some investigations, although other studies report lower correlations, averaging .5, between IQ in adolescence and adult occupational status (Rutter, 1989). At first glance these results seems to confirm that IQ scores are fairly good predictors of later success. However, a closer examination of the facts reveals a different and more complicated picture, suggesting that the correlations reflect the influence of factors other than IQ, such as schooling and social class. For example, if both schooling and socioeconomic class are held constant, so that their possible influence is ruled out, and the correlation between IQ and later success is then calculated, the proportion of the variability in people's economic success that is predicted by variations in their IQs becomes negligible (see Lewontin, 1982). In other words, IQ on its own is not a good predictor of success. This result suggests that the fact that economic success and IQ are correlated is simply an outcome of IQ being related to other influences that do contribute to individuals' success.

Some other findings from the same study illustrate the relative importance of someone's IQ score and his or her social background as predictors of his or her eventual success in life. In men with average IQs, those who came from the highest socioeconomic classes were over seven times more likely to end up receiving high incomes than were men with the same IQs who started life in poor families. In addition, when men with average IQs who received high amounts of schooling were compared with men having similar IQs but who had received very little schooling, it turned out that the former were more than 10 times as likely as the latter to be earning very high incomes.

Clearly, in some circumstances IQ scores appear to be reasonably good predictors, but only because they are correlated with other influences that are better predictors. In fairness, however, it is equally true that there are certain situations in which IQs are moderately good predictors of social outcomes even when other variables such as social class are held constant.[1]

Because social class affects IQ scores, the practice of requiring successful applicants to have high IQ scores either as an admission requirement in education or as a criterion in selection for employment can result in unfair discrimination against minorities and the poor. This is especially true when, as is often the case, the predictive value of IQ scores is either nil or too small to make a real contribution to estimating an individual's chances of succeeding. All that is achieved here by insisting on minimal IQ scores is the creation of a barrier that arbitrarily excludes certain groups of people. This is especially likely to happen when entry requirements come to be regarded as an indication of the quality of people admitted to a profession. For example, graduate programmes in universities may insist on candidates for admission having very high scores at cognitive tests, although it is known that students' levels of success at a programme are unrelated to those scores. This somewhat absurd and discriminatory state of affairs may be maintained simply because it is feared that the prestige of a programme would diminish were it to become known that students with low test scores have been admitted to it (see, for example, Sternberg and Williams, forthcoming).

High IQ and High Achievement: The Terman Study

Until now, this chapter has been mainly concerned with the extent to which IQ scores predict various kinds of success in individuals of average or near-average levels of ability. Now we turn to highly intelligent individuals. How useful is it to administer intelligence tests to people with high levels of intellectual ability?

The findings of a large-scale investigation that began in the earlier days of intelligence testing appeared to show that intelligence tests could be a powerful tool for identifying children who would grow up to be high-achieving adults. In the early 1920s, Lewis Terman identified a large sample of 1,500 children in California who on the basis of their IQ scores and other measures were estimated to be within the most intelligent 1 per cent of their generation. Their IQs averaged around 150. Terman and his colleagues kept in touch with most of these children over the ensuing years, for as many as five decades in some cases. A large-scale long-term study of this kind seems to provide an excellent test of the predictive value of intelligence testing among highly able individuals.

Some of the findings of Terman's investigation appeared to prove that IQ scores are excellent instruments for identifying future high achievers. For example, at school the young people he identified were well ahead of the average, their health was above average, and they tended to be good at sports. Most of them appeared to be mature and well-adjusted individuals. As they developed they continued to make above-average progress. Seventy per cent of them gained a university or college degree, nearly 10 times the proportion of young people graduating in the general population at that time. Even compared with other graduates they did exceptionally well, with five times as many of Terman's group gaining PhDs. Their average occupational status was well above the mean, and a large proportion became scientists, writers, or business executives. Their income levels were also considerably above average. They were happier than average. They even lived longer.

But as a testament to the value of IQ testing, Terman's findings are not quite as impressive as they first appear to be. It now appears that it would have been possible to make almost equally accurate predictions about the young people's futures in the absence of any intelligence test scores. The children selected for the study were different from the average not only in their intelligence levels. Many of them came from relatively prosperous families, for example, and had parents in the professions. Information about the parents' educational levels and their social and economic status would have yielded equally valid predictions concerning the young people's eventual achievements (Ceci, 1990; Sorokin, 1956). Had children from a range of social backgrounds comparable to those of the participants in Terman's study been taken at random, they would have been practically as successful, on average, as Terman's children turned out to be. In fact, a sociologist who examined the data from the study concluded that if children from social classes equivalent to those of the participants in Terman's study had been selected on the basis of their school marks and teachers' evaluations, but without using intelligence tests at all, the proportion of them who would have had unusually successful adult careers would have actually been higher than the proportion of the individuals actually identified in the investigation by Terman (Sorokin, 1956).

In the later part of his career, Terman did appreciate that it was wrong to compare the individuals in his sample with people taken at random, because of the important differences between them in their backgrounds and social class. He reported, however, that his high-IQ individuals were not only more successful than people on average, but they also ended up with higher incomes and higher-status positions than other university graduates. However, even that finding does not necessarily make the case for IQ tests appreciably more convincing. There are two reasons why. In the first place, the differences between Terman's subjects and other graduates were either small or – with some of the chosen criteria for success – nil. Secondly, as Stephen Ceci (1990) has noted, using unselected graduates as a comparison group was inappropriate. Terman's participants differed from them in a number of crucial ways. For example, Terman's subjects came from wealthier and better-connected families, and unlike the other graduates they had repeatedly been told that they were unusually intelligent and encouraged to believe that they could do well.

So it would appear that there is nothing uniquely powerful about test scores as predictors. Saying that does not mean denying that IQ scores are any use at all for making estimates about the future success about high achievers; however, other kinds of information can do that job equally well. In the particular case of the children studied by Terman, the fact that they came from advantaged backgrounds made a big contribution to their success in life, and it also contributed to their high intelligence test scores.

Other findings from Terman's study suggest that in a group of people who all have high IQs, knowing their exact scores does not help to predict which individuals among them will be the highest achievers. Thus when Terman compared the 150 most successful men in his study with the 150 least successful, he found that there was no difference between them in their average childhood IQs. Yet the differences between the two groups in real-life outcomes were very substantial. In the first group, the majority were happy and prosperous, and enjoyed fulfilling lives, whereas personal and professional failures were far more common in the second group.

If IQ differences did not contribute to the varying lifetime success of individual men within Terman's sample, what *were* the causes? Terman's investigation was not designed to answer that question, but the data yield a number of clues. Comparing the above two groups, who formed the top 20 per cent (group A) and the bottom 20 per cent (group C) of the sample in terms of lifetime success, there are a number of interesting differences. Virtually all the men in group A but only 17 per cent in group C came from professional or business families, and the group A families were also better educated and more prosperous. There were differences in family lifestyles, as is indicated by the fact that many more of the group A men played tennis, whereas men in group C were more likely to spend their leisure time watching football and baseball.

In short, there were large differences between the groups in their families' cultural lifestyles. These determine the experiences, opportunities, role models, and expectations that are available to a child. Families also act in different ways as support systems, with educated and prosperous families better equipped to take advantage of various kinds of know-how and social networks that can be counted upon in order to help a young man to find his way. As we discovered in Chapter 4, in looking for causes of race differences in test scores, there are major differences in the extent to which the culture of a child's family life can help to give a child self-confidence and the expectation of succeeding. Families also differ greatly in their effectiveness at providing opportunities to gain vital knowledge and skills.

The cultural differences between the backgrounds of group A and group C individuals almost certainly contributed to their contrasting lives and careers. Despite all having the impressive mental abilities that were reflected in their high childhood IQs, these individuals' chances of enjoying a productive and successful adult life were strongly influenced by the support that they were given throughout their early years, within their differing family surroundings.

Influences Outside the Family

Family backgrounds are not the only source of variation in the opportunities, experiences, and expectations that can influence an individual's career. Another important factor is schooling. Physical location is yet another: the experiences of a young person growing up in a poor rural area are not the same as those of a child living in a city. It is no coincidence that Nobel prizewinners have tended to come from prosperous urban regions, where music, science, and the arts are on offer (Berry, 1981). Incidentally, there were no Nobelists among Terman's

California sample, although two individuals who were rejected because their IQs were too low did win Nobel prizes (Ceci, 1990).

Yet another influence is the time in history during which a person's formative years are spent. Glenn Elder, a sociologist, looked at some of the ways in which this affected the lives of people in Terman's sample of highly intelligent individuals (Elder, 1986). Elder selected two groups of men with average IQs. The first group consisted of men born between 1904 and 1910, and the second comprised men born between 1911 and 1917. Compared with the latter group, men in the former group suffered in two important ways. First, they reached adulthood during a severe and long-lasting depression, and, secondly, many of them had their lives disrupted by World War II, at around the time their careers were beginning to take off. Elder found that in a large proportion of the men he studied, their lives were indeed affected by these events. The period in which they were born was a major determinant of important indicators of lifetime success, such as income and professional status.

For much of this century it has been almost universally assumed that the long-term investigation that Lewis Terman initiated demonstrated the remarkable power of the IQ measure to predict high achievement in life. With hindsight it is clear that the actual story is very different. Although it is true that having a high childhood IQ is a moderately good predictor of success in adulthood, to a considerable extent that is only because high IQ is associated with other important influences. IQ alone, when other contributing factors are controlled, is a weak predictor.

Conclusion

We have seen that the findings of a number of inquiries based on the data collected by Terman and his co-researchers agree in showing that within a group of highly intelligent individuals differences in their IQs make little or no contribution to their lifetime success. But that does not mean that test scores are never useful. As the findings reported earlier in the chapter make clear, in a random sample of individuals, having a greater diversity of IQs than Terman's subjects, IQ scores do provide a basis for making predictions. How helpful those predictions are depends upon the circumstances. On the one hand, the predictive power of IQ tests is not usually sufficient to make a real difference in the accuracy of estimates of the future success of individuals. On the other hand, test scores can be useful in circumstances that require large numbers of people being selected for roles that demand a fair degree of mental ability. That is especially true when the selectors have no other information about applicants' capabilities.

Note

1. Herrnstein and Murray (1994) provide numerous instances.

7

Genetics and Intelligence

That people's lives are differently affected by their genes is apparent when we see the reaction to a beautiful young woman entering a restaurant. Eyes turn towards her and waiters smile and rush to help, but the person who follows her into the restaurant gets a different response. That example illustrates just one of many ways in which genetic differences between people contribute to the fact that two individuals can occupy the identical place at the same time, and yet experience it very differently. A child living in Nazi Germany is spat upon because she is Jewish. A black American is spurned by bigots who believe that blacks are lazy. For both these individuals, genetics will have influenced the life that is experienced. And because people's activities are affected by the manner in which others respond to them, it is not unlikely that over a period of time the knowledge and skills that an individual gains may also be affected by that person's genetic composition. In short, differences between people in a variety of genetically influenced characteristics do contribute to their lives being experienced differently, with outcomes that can often affect IQ scores. A consequence is that inherited differences between people have a part to play among the numerous influences that lead to individuals varying in their levels of intelligence.

Direct and Indirect Genetic Influences

In principle, genetic influences could affect intelligence either directly or indirectly, or in both of these ways. These different ways in which genetic differences between people may conceivably affect their IQ scores are often confused, and it is not always clear which one a writer on intelligence has in mind. But they need to be disentangled, because their practical implications are very different.

The possibility that genetic variability between people might affect intelligence directly, just as genes determine the colour of a person's eyes, is implied by the familiar idea that it may become possible to identify certain 'genes for intelligence', or to locate genetic 'blueprints' that help fix a person's intelligence. According to that view, genetically related individuals are more similar to each other than people selected at random in the extent to which they possess some characteristic that directly affects each person's level of intelligence. For instance, it is conceivable that there exist genetically determined differences between people in the speed at which certain mental operations are performed, or, as Spearman believed, in some kind of mental force or energy. Writers within the intelligence theory and psychometric tradition often appear to take it for granted that differences between people in their intelligence are directly linked to genetic sources of variability.

The alternative possibility is that genetic differences have consequences that can lead to individual differences in IQ scores, but work indirectly. Numerous personal attributes can have effects that may influence IQ levels. These range from mood, temperament, and personality variables to factors such as self-confidence, competitiveness, enthusiasm, attentiveness, and so on. Each of these influences can affect a person's behaviour, and make it more or less likely that that individual will engage in activities that enable mental skills and knowledge to be acquired, thus making the person more intelligent. And in the case of each it is possible that the reason why they vary from person to person is partly a consequence of genetic differences between individuals. In that event it would be entirely possible that differences between people in any of a number of the dimensions on which they differ genetically could – in at least some circumstances – lead to outcomes that would affect a person's score at an intelligence test. Note that this would happen even if the dimensions of variability were not at all directly related to intelligence as such.

It is important to make the distinction between direct and indirect genetic influences on intelligence, and to establish whether there is evidence for both of these possibilities, or only one of them, because the two have vastly different practical implications for human lives. If the existence of direct influences was verified, it would follow that, in line with the views of intelligence theorists, a person's intelligence is relatively fixed from birth and that IQs could not be greatly modified by non-genetic influences and interventions. However, as we shall see, if it were to be established that genetic differences between people have only indirect effects on their intelligence, many of those effects would not be at all inevitable. There would be considerable room for the possibility of appropriate interventions reducing or even nullifying the impact of genetic differences between individuals.

When an influence is indirect rather than direct, its actual impact, if there is to be one, depends upon numerous other circumstances. The possible effects of genetic variability on intelligence might be not unlike those of a nation's mineral wealth on national prosperity. Take coal in Britain, for instance. For millions of years Britain has had abundant stocks of coal, but prior to the Industrial Revolution there were few opportunities for people to benefit from that resource. However, by the eighteenth century industry was becoming increasingly able to profit from coal, and by the nineteenth century the explosion of uses for coal together with vastly improved facilities for extracting and transporting it resulted in it being a major determinant of the nation's wealth. By the late twentieth century the importance of coal had receded, however, partly as a result of the increasing use of alternative sources of power.

So the response to a question about the importance of coal in Britain's national prosperity would have to include a phrase like 'it depends upon . . .'. There have been times when it has been extremely important, but there have also been times when it has made little if any impact. At any particular moment, the extent to which the resources that coal provides have actually made a difference have depended on various other circumstances.

The same is broadly true whenever indirect sources of influence are present. That is, other circumstances largely dictate the magnitude of the effects, or whether there are to be any substantial effects at all. That is certainly the case with indirect genetic influences upon human intelligence levels.

Although it is often taken for granted that at least some differences between individuals in intelligence are directly rather than indirectly connected to differences in their genes, there is absolutely no firm evidence that this is the case. All the research findings that may appear to point to the possibility of direct genetic influences on intelligence are equally consistent with the view that any links that do exist between genetic variability and IQ scores are indirect ones. Moreover, most of the research findings that have been introduced to support the view that such links exist take the form of demonstrations that there are similarities between people for which there appears to be no alternative explanation, other than a genetic one. In other words, a genetic cause of intelligence is inferred to be present, not because there is positive evidence of it but simply because there seems to be a lack of alternative explanations of observed similarities between biologically related people.

Very little is known about the precise nature of the genetic mechanisms that contribute to the fact that people differ in their intelligence. Almost nothing is known about the chains of events via which their supposed influences operate. Indeed, it is hard to see how that knowledge can ever be made available whilst there is no agreed-upon precise definition of intelligence and the question of what intelligence actually is remains unresolved. In the absence of a proper definition of intelligence, the task that needs to be done is literally impossible, in the same way that planning a route to Eldorado would be impossible. For the reasons that make it impossible to decide how to reach a place that has an unknown location and which may not even exist at all, it is simply impossible to specify all the contributing influences that lead to an undefined end product.

Broadly speaking, the outcomes of indirect influences are more uncertain, and the likely effects are easier to modify or eliminate, than is the case with the outcomes of direct influences. Is that true of intelligence? Are there good reasons for believing that whereas a direct connection between genes and IQ would mean genetically favoured people inevitably having an advantage over others, if only indirect links are involved it is possible that appropriate interventions can remove or reduce any such advantage?

A simple illustration will be helpful here, demonstrating that when causation is indirect its effects are often far from inevitable. Imagine a situation in which men live in an outdoor prison surrounded by a 6-foot wall. It is discovered that half of the prisoners become expert ornithologists, knowledgeable about bird life, and that the men's degree of ornithological expertise is linked to their genetic inheritance. How did this come about? At first, the only possible explanation for these observations seems to be that a person's biology directly determines his or her ornithological capability, with people being either born or not born to know about birds. And nothing, it appears, can be done to change that situation.

Later, however, the real reason for the connection is revealed. It turns out to reside in the fact that men who can see over the fence surrounding the prison have a much better chance of learning about birds than those who cannot. In other words, a man's ornithological knowledge is linked to his height. Once that is established, it is easy to think of ways to help those who have been genetically disadvantaged (by their limited height) for acquiring ornithological expertise. For example, simply standing on a box or some steps would largely wipe out the cause of variability in people's ornithological knowledge. So a simple environmental intervention eliminates the differences in knowledge, despite the fact that those differences undoubtedly had genetic origins, beginning as they did with inherited differences in men's height.

There is no guarantee that it will always be possible to intervene in ways that eliminate those differences in people's capabilities that are an indirect consequence of genetic variability, but in many realistic circumstances this definitely can be done. To take another example, discovering a large group of people in whom it has been established, first, that about one person in two has learned to read, and, secondly, that a genetic link is involved, with ability to read running in members of the same family, even when they are separated. Here again, as in the previous illustration, one's first impulse is to assume that since the reading difficulties are genetically caused, that is simply that, in which event all that can be done is to sympathize with those unfortunates who are not innately endowed to read. But as in the previous example, the initial conclusion is quickly seen to be in error. In the present case the mistake becomes apparent when it is discovered that there is a more immediate cause of some individuals failing to learn to read. This time the immediate reason is that, for genetic reasons, some people have poor eyesight. As soon as that is known, it becomes clear that an effective intervention is possible, in the form of spectacles. Giving eyeglasses to those children who need them has the effect of eradicating the genetically caused differences between people in their ability to read.

Heritability

It is often believed that the abilities to which genes make a contribution are determined in advance and are therefore outside our control, but the above examples contradict that view. As Robert Plomin (1986) has noted, the more that is known about the nature of any genetic influences that affect a human trait, the more likely it is that intervention or prevention strategies can be devised. There is nothing at all inevitable about the consequences of genetic differences.

Measures of the 'heritability' of traits can provide a useful indication of the influence genetics has on variation in a trait within a specific population living in a particular environment (Alland, 1996). Estimates of the heritability of intelligence have varied from study to study, from .4 or less to as much as .7. However, as Charles Locurto (1991) and others have pointed out, knowing a trait's heritability does not make it possible to know what will happen in the future, after environmental changes have taken place. And contrary to what is widely assumed, heritability is not a measure of the extent to which a quality is genetic. An attribute can be the outcome of exclusively genetic causes and yet have a zero heritability, as in the case with eye-colour in a population within which everyone has blue eyes.

Also, because heritability is an indicator of the proportion of the relative variance of the environmental and genetic contributions, high heritability actually implies favourable environmental circumstances. That is because in those circumstances in which all individuals have good opportunities to learn, genetic differences will be a major influence on individuals' capabilities. In less favourable circumstances heritability will be lower. For this reason, some studies have found the heritability of intelligence among people living in affluent white American suburbs to be appreciably higher than among the inhabitants of urban ghettos (Brace, 1996).

Genetic Influences: Facts and Fallacies

Some widely accepted beliefs about inheritance are simply wrong. For example, there is no truth at all in the often-stated view that genes fix a person's 'potential', as is implied by the metaphor that depicts people's intelligence levels as being analogous to buckets that can be more and less full (depending on environmental influences) but have limits imposed by the (genetically determined) size of the bucket. Another common misconception is that genes operate as straightforward instructions that command the organism how to operate itself, as is suggested by familiar metaphors in which the genes are depicted as operating like recipes or knitting instructions. It is more realistic to imagine genetic elements as being parts of a complex system that has a number of different levels and stages, with the various parts influencing one another in complicated ways. The implications of this complex set of circumstances for intelligence have been addressed in a forthcoming book by Ken Richardson. As in other complicated systems, such as the economy of a nation, it would be wrong to assume that it is always possible to locate *the* causes of the existing state of affairs. In the case of a nation's economic health it is clear that numerous factors enter into the equation – wage levels, unemployment, inflation, training, money supply, and so on – but equally clear that each of these not only affects the others but is influenced by them. Because of that, the job of creating a healthy economy is a complicated balancing act in which various interacting influences have to be taken into account. It is similar with genetic causation: identifying *the* gene or genes that result in a person achieving a given level of intelligence is not a realistic possibility.

Because genetic sources of individual variability do not exert their influences through straightforward chains of causes and effects, the eventual consequences of a person's possessing particular genetic characteristics may be unpredictable. Few traits are firmly fixed by a person's genes. Take a characteristic like fatness, for instance. It is possible to identify people who, for partly genetic reasons, will tend to be fatter than average when there is a high level of nutrition. But the same person may be thinner than average when nutrition levels are low

(Lewontin, 1982). Here the same genetic materials can help make someone fat or thin, depending on the circumstances. Similarly, a characteristic that is partly inherited may lead to a person doing better than someone else in some circumstances but worse in others. Also, predicting outcomes on the basis of a knowledge of individuals' genetic endowment is made even more difficult by the fact that the most favourable environment for maximizing the development of an organism with a particular genetic make-up will not be the most effective environment for a genetically different individual.

Even when a personal characteristic is highly heritable, that does not make it unchangeable. Stephen Jay Gould (1984) illustrates this point by examining some influences on body height. He imagines that the average height of adult males in a poor Indian village beset with nutritional deprivation is 5 feet 6 inches, with even the tallest fathers being no more than around 5 feet 8. Since height is highly heritable, tall fathers will tend to have tall sons and short fathers will tend to have short sons. Yet with improved nutrition it may be possible in a few generations to increase the average height to over 5 feet 10 inches, higher than the tallest first-generation fathers, despite the substantial heritability of height.

It is also important to remember the information yielded by calculations of the heritability of a characteristic – the degree to which variability between people in that trait is associated with genetic variability – is descriptive and not predictive. That is to say, a measure of a trait's heritability only purports to indicate what happened in a particular sample of people living in their particular circumstances. It does not place restrictions on what can or might happen in the future, in changed circumstances. To assume otherwise would be rather like planning modern farming on the basis of nineteenth-century statistics concerning the implications for milk production of having different genetic strains of cattle and different kinds of food. Increasing scientific knowledge of nutrition has made old information obsolete and no longer applicable; we now have new and better ways to improve nutrition. For similar reasons, it is possible that estimates of the heritability of intelligence that were obtained in the past may be inapplicable in the present and the future because they were obtained in circumstances in which, through ignorance or lack of educational facilities, the efforts made to stimulate children's mental development environmentally were ineffective or half-hearted.

Another limitation of estimates of heritability stems from the evidence that they have been based upon. For instance, because the adoptive homes in those adoption studies that have contributed the research data have tended to be similar to one another in the degree to which they provided environments that succeeded in stimulating mental development, it is possible that the data yielded by these studies may have under-represented the range of differences that can occur between children in their everyday experiences. As a result, basing conclusions on evidence provided by those studies could be misleading. It could be like deciding after an investigation of cake-making that the effects of varying the number of eggs on the taste and texture of a cake are small, while neglecting to note that none of the cakes actually tasted in the study had contained more than four eggs or less than three. Had cakes containing only one egg or as many as six eggs been examined, the conclusions about the importance of the number of eggs in a cake might have been very different. Similarly with the adoption studies: had the adoptive parents varied more in the extent to which they provided children with learning experiences, the authors' conclusions might have given more weight to the importance of environmental influences and less to that of genetic variability. Now that we have been made aware of the immense positive benefits of providing a child with a good learning environment, with many people becoming better informed about effective ways to achieve this, it is likely that in a random sample of children the variability in the extent to which their early learning environments are stimulating and supportive will be greater than in the past. This is likely to result in environmental differences between children being a more substantial cause of individual differences in intelligence than formerly.

The eggs-in-a-cake metaphor provides a reminder of another basic but neglected fact. When outcomes are the result of a number of interacting causes it is rarely possible to quantify the importance of each one of the different contributing influences. We cannot say that the taste of a cake depends to X per cent on the number of eggs, Y per cent on the amount of flour, and Z per cent on the other ingredients. The effects of the various components are not additive. As in a chemical reaction, when elements combine they do so in ways that cannot be calculated from entering their quantities into a simple algorithm. It is similar with human abilities. Even when it is clear that people differ for reasons that are partly genetic and partly reflect differences in individuals' experiences, it may be impossible to quantify the relative importance of the different influences.

Evidence from Twin Studies

Despite all the problems I have raised, there is almost universal agreement among intelligence experts who follow a psychometric approach that differences between people in intelligence are largely inherited. They base this conclusion mainly on the findings of studies of identical twins who have been brought up separately. The reasoning behind these investigations is that if identical twins who are reared apart nevertheless resemble each other in intelligence, that cannot be due to similarities in their environments or in their experiences; it must be caused by the fact that the twins share identical genes. Another finding, that identical twins reared apart are more similar in their intelligence levels than non-identical twins reared apart, gives further support for this view, since non-identical twins, unlike identical twins, do not have the same genetic materials.

The results of investigations undertaken with identical twins demonstrate that identical twins reared apart do indeed have similar IQs. What is more, the reduced similarity of IQ scores in identical twins brought up apart compared with identical twins reared together is substantially less than the difference in similarity that is found when identical twins are compared with non-identical twins. That pattern of results shows, it is claimed, that manipulating genetic similarity whilst keeping environmental similarity constant has a substantial influence upon scores, whereas the effects of doing the reverse are smaller. These findings are seen as providing firm empirical evidence that differences in intelligence are largely inherited.

It would be hard to argue with that conclusion if there were no flaws in the investigations yielding the findings. But although in principle it is possible to design and undertake studies in which the intelligence test scores obtained by identical twins yield clear evidence concerning the possibility of intelligence being largely inherited, in practice that would be very difficult, and perhaps impossible. As we shall discover in the following section, the research that has actually been done is defective in a number of ways. Because of that it is doubtful whether findings from the majority of studies that have been conducted with twins can provide firm answers to questions about the heritability of intelligence. An especially important limitation of these investigations is that the measures of the intelligence of identical twins reared apart were obtained from children who were not actually reared entirely apart at all.

Consider how a satisfactory investigation might be devised. To start with, it would be necessary to have a large sample of identical twins. It would be helpful if their eventual distribution of intelligence test scores broadly matched that of the population in general. It would also be useful to know the intelligence test scores of their biological parents.

Secondly, it would be necessary to have the twins in each pair totally separated. The only entirely satisfactory way to ensure that they do not share common experiences would be to divide the emerging embryos immediately after conception, and rear them entirely apart. In fact that is simply impossible for a number of reasons, and the nearest approximation to it that can be achieved in practice is to separate the twins at birth. However, it is important to acknowledge that even an investigation in which twins are separated at birth is not the same as one in which the twins are reared *completely* apart, since twins who share a prenatal environment will have experienced a shared environment for nine crucial formative months of their lives. It is well known that the ways in which children's prenatal environments differ can have powerful effects on postnatal development. A child's intelligence may be affected by maternal smoking and drinking during pregnancy and by various other characteristics of the pregnant mother.[1] Consequently, no two individuals who began life in the identical uterus can be said to have been reared apart to the extent that would be essential in order for an investigation based on separated twins to yield entirely unambiguous evidence about the effects of genes on intelligence. In practice, however, separation at birth is the best that can be done.

Thirdly, if it is not possible to obtain genetically related individuals who have not shared a prenatal environment, it is essential to keep strictly to the next-best option, which is to use children who have been separated immediately after birth. Because non-identical twins as well as identical ones share prenatal environments (which is fortunate, from a research viewpoint), providing that twins are separated as soon as they are born it is meaningful to compare the average difference in IQ between identical twins reared together and apart (from birth onwards) with the difference between non-identical twins reared together and apart. If we were to find that identical twins reared entirely apart had very similar IQs, but that this was not true of non-identical twins reared apart, that would be strong evidence of a genetic contribution to IQ scores.

However, for such comparisons to be valid it would be vital to ensure that the separation did take place immediately after birth. In addition, it would be important to be sure that the twins had no contact with each other and had no knowledge of one another. It is also important that the adoptive parents knew nothing about the children's natural parents and were given no information about their biological backgrounds.

Fourthly, there would have to be a satisfactory way of allocating children to adoptive parents. The choice of an appropriate procedure would depend upon the precise questions that the investigation was designed to answer. One possible procedure would be to allocate the children to adoptive parents entirely at random, having ensured in advance that the distribution of the sample of individuals providing the adoptive parents matched the distribution of the population in general geographically, culturally, and economically, and that the distribution of the adoptive parents' IQs also matched that of the broader population. Allocating children in this way would help to ensure that the indications of the possible influence of genes on the children who participated in the study were representative of the state of affairs currently existing in the broader population within which the study was undertaken.

An alternative possibility would be to allocate children at random to adoptive parents from each of two groups, one comprising highly intelligent and well-educated individuals who had demonstrated themselves to be able and prepared to offer to a child an especially supportive and stimulating family background throughout the years of childhood, and the other made up of individuals whose IQs were low and who had shown themselves to be ill equipped to provide an optimal intellectual environment for a child's formative years. Allocating the children to adoptive parents in that manner would enable the investigation to provide data relating to a different but equally interesting question. In that case the study would be assessing the likely effects of genetic differences in circumstances where differences between children in their early experiences varied to a greater extent than is typical at present. Whereas the first design would yield findings indicating the relative extents to which genetic and environmental determinants currently contribute to children's measured intelligence in the general population, the second one would help make it possible to estimate what might happen in the future, at a time when there is more widespread awareness of the need to maximize children's experiences.

Limitations of Twin Studies

Studies conducted on the lines I have indicated would undoubtedly be capable of yielding valuable information about genetic contributions to differences between people in measured intelligence. There would be some limitations. For example, the findings would not provide any indication of the extent to which genetic effects on intelligence are direct or indirect. Also, there would be some uncertainties concerning the applicability of evidence based on twins to non-twins, simply because the lives of identical twins are different from those of other people. For instance, when two twins are in the same uterus they may compete for resources, leading to substantial differences in body weight. When that happens, the twin with the higher body weight tends to have higher intelligence than the twin with low body weight.

In fact, however, most of the studies that have been conducted using identical twins to investigate the possible contribution of genetic differences to variability in intelligence fall short of meeting all four of the essential conditions I have outlined. That is, first, they are not based upon adequate population samples; secondly, they (perhaps inevitably) do not incorporate prenatal separation; thirdly, when separation has taken place following birth it has not been immediate; and, fourthly, allocation of children to adoptive parents has often been highly selective, and far from being either systematic or random, as would be desirable in a well-designed research investigation.

By and large, the studies have been defective not because the researchers have been less than competent at designing and undertaking investigations but because practical constraints have got in the way. What would have been desirable from a research viewpoint has often been prevented by the realities of the world we live in. For a start, serious problems are created by the fact that identical twins who are not brought up by their mothers are very rare. For good humanitarian reasons, when it is inevitable that twins have to be reared apart from their mother, efforts are normally made to make sure that they are kept together rather than being separated. When it has been impossible to avoid a degree of separation, the chances are that both members of a pair of twins will have been brought up in similar circumstances, often by different members of the same family, and will have had a certain amount of contact with each other during childhood.

Consequently, the situation that would be most desirable from a research point of view, involving having identical twins separated at birth and brought up with no contact with one another, is one which, nowadays at least, social agencies and the children's families strive hard to avoid. It is therefore very difficult indeed to locate suitable participants for research that depends upon having a sample of identical twins who have been brought up apart. In the rare circumstances where that is possible, there is likely to be a lack of accurate documentation concerning, for example, the time when they were first separated, the circumstances in which they were reared during their early years and the frequency and length of occasions when they were together during their childhoods. At the time when an investigation is being conducted, which may be 30 or more years after the birth of the twins, much of this information may be unavailable, except in the unreliable memories of elderly relatives. In the twins' childhood years, ensuring that accurate records would be available for researchers in the distant future would have been the last thing on the minds of anyone concerned with their upbringing.

All these reasons have stood in the way of effective investigations of the intelligence of identical twins separated at birth. The total number of pairs of separated identical twins participating in the major studies has been insufficient for it to be possible to have samples which match the general population in important respects. In many cases it is uncertain exactly when the twins were separated, how much of their time they were apart, and how many contacts they had with one another. Often, detailed information about these important events is simply not available, and when it does exist its reliability and accuracy may be questionable. Only in extremely few cases is it possible to be certain that a particular pair of twins were separated in the first weeks after birth and that the children had no contact with each other throughout their childhoods.

Because of these limitations in the data that are available, researchers have had to cut corners. For instance, instead of comparing twins reared together with twins reared entirely apart, they have compared twins together with twins reared partly apart. But that is a very different comparison, and the difference has important (but often unacknowledged) implications for the manner in which the findings should be interpreted, and for the estimation of heritability. In some cases twins that were supposed to have been reared apart actually spent very substantial portions of their childhoods together, making it possible that they could have shared many early environmental influences, a fact that has major implications for heritability estimates. Some twin researchers, notably Thomas Bouchard and his co-researchers, (Bouchard et al., 1990) assert that this is not a problem because correlations between differences in twins' intelligence levels and amount of time they have spent apart are not significant. That argument would be convincing if one could be absolutely sure of the accuracy of the information about the twins' early lives. But because the actual circumstances in which siblings are separated are not usually ones in which it is possible to provide the day-to-day documentation that would be necessary for establishing all the relevant facts, it is likely that most of the assessments of the degree of separation in early life have been somewhat crude at best. As it happens, there is clear evidence that correlations in twins' IQs do reduce when the similarities of their environments are reduced. For instance, in one study of 40 pairs of twins, the correlation in IQs among those who were raised by branches of the same family was .83, but in those twins who were raised by completely different families and had attended different schools the correlation was only .47, thus accounting for only a quarter of the variability in their intelligence (Locurto, 1991: 116).

Another problem with twin studies as sources of evidence concerning possible genetic links is that they fail to take into account some of the emotional antecedents and consequences of being an adopted child. Identical twins reared apart are unlike other people in a number of respects that may strongly affect their early experiences. First, for example, the sheer fact that twins know they are twins may influence them. Secondly, they have been separated from their parents and from their siblings, and that experience will almost certainly have had long-lasting effects on their lives. Thirdly, their adoptive parents and other significant adults will be aware of these facts, which may affect their own responses to the twins.

It is hard to specify the extent to which the validity of estimates of the heritability of human intelligence that have emerged from studies of identical twins is compromised by the limitations and deficiencies of twin studies. Failures to take full account of these problems has very probably led to some published estimates overestimating the true levels of heritability in the general population. All the same, since individuals are affected in so many ways by their genes, albeit often indirectly and probabalistically rather than inevitably, in most existing circumstances the true heritability of intelligence in human populations is almost certainly above zero.

Conclusion

In this chapter we have seen that whilst it is certainly true that individuals are differently affected by their genetic make-up, the influence of genetic differences on intelligence levels is neither as straightforward nor as inevitable as it is often assumed to be. In particular, because the ways in which genetic differences between people can influence their IQs are indirect rather than direct, there are numerous opportunities for making interventions that can prevent the potentially harmful consequences for some individuals of genetic differences between people. So far as intelligence is concerned, genetic sources of variability do not have consequences that are written in stone, and genes do not act as blueprints that directly fix a person's level of intelligence. Nor is there a 'gene for intelligence' that determines a person's IQ. Estimates of the heritability of intelligence have been based on studies of identical twins that are defective in ways that make it necessary to question the validity of the conclusions.

Note

1. I am indebted to Dr George Mandler for drawing my attention to J.O. Davis, J.A. Phelps, and H.S. Brancha's 1995 study: 'Prenatal development of monozygotic twins and concordance for schizophrenia', in *Schizophrenia Bulletin*, 21: 357–66. These authors examined concordance for schizophrenia in monozygotic twins. This is around 50 per cent, on average, and 60 per cent in twins who developed prenatally in separate placentas. However, when the authors measured the degree of concordance in those monozygotic twins who had separate placentas (known as monochorionic pairs) the concordance reduced to only 11 per cent. This strongly suggests that the degree of similarity in monozygotic twins in their vulnerability to schizophrenia is largely due to their shared prenatal environment rather than to the genetic similarity that the high concordance ratings appear to indicate. If that finding is at all applicable to other qualities that are regarded as being highly heritable, it may indicate that many of the identical twin similarities that appear to point to high heritability are actually caused by similarity in prenatal environments.

8

Newer Approaches to Intelligence

As we have seen, there have been many criticisms of the intelligence theory approach, according to which intelligence is not only a product of mental activity but also the underlying reason why some people are highly intelligent. Responses to such criticisms have typically included a demand that the challenger reveal just what it is that makes some people more intelligent than others, if not the presence of an underlying quality of intelligence, which is the preferred answer of Spearman and the followers in his tradition.

In fact, as we have seen, there are numerous possible contributing causes to one individual being more intelligent than another. It is almost certainly wrong to think that all that is wrong with intelligence theory is that it offers an incorrect solution to a well-defined question. The problems go further. The kinds of questions posed by intelligence theorists may be simply inappropriate ones for generating explorations of the causes of individual differences in people's mental abilities.

That possibility, which encourages the suggestion that traditional approaches to intelligence may need to be replaced with very different ones that do not even tackle the same questions, is raised by glancing at the activities of scientists attempting to create 'artificial intelligence' in computers. One of their aims has been to manufacture computer systems that operate in ways that simulate human intelligence. Intelligent systems, like people, process information, adapt and change in ways that make use of memory and acquired knowledge, make decisions, and so on.

A revealing fact emerging from artificial intelligence systems is that attempts to examine them with a view to trying to locate within them some unitary underlying quality or process that corresponds even remotely to intelligence processes envisaged as the mental energy thought to be encapsulated in Spearman's *g* prove totally fruitless. It is equally unrewarding to ask the developers of artificial intelligence systems to identify the single source of their effectiveness, the one element or parameter that makes one artificial intelligence system more effective – more 'intelligent' – than another. That simply cannot be done. What is more, many of the developers of artificial intelligence systems would consider the very idea absurd, just as it would be absurd to look for the single quality that makes an engine powerful, or for the one process that makes an economy healthy, or creates a sunny day in December, or the unitary mechanism that is responsible for making certain individuals charming.

Searching for the one secret of success behind the achievements of a complicated system usually proves to be a vain endeavour. That is especially likely in connection with human intelligence, because of the vast complexity of the computational system that creates intelligent behaviour, the human brain. A number of scientists have commented on the sheer implausibility of the belief that it might be possible to identify within the mental mechanisms underlying human cognition any common element or common process where the cause of variability in intelligence can be seen to reside. As an explanation of differing intelligence levels, that is too crude a possibility to be a realistic one. It takes no account of what is known about the extremely complicated and sophisticated ways in which human brains actually generate intelligent behaviour.

Only a few newer approaches have had substantial impacts on thinking about intelligence. That is not because the traditional intelligence theory approach has gone uncriticized. However, not all the alternative ideas proposed by those who have identified defects in intelligence theory have taken the form of new theories of intelligence, as such. Some of those researchers who have investigated the origins on intelligent behaviours have ignored traditional intelligence theory altogether. For example, a number of them have chosen to investigate the causes of intellectual competence within the developmental framework pioneered by Piaget. These researchers have concentrated on the children's acquisition of intelligence without being greatly concerned about individual differences. Other researchers have examined the growth of mental abilities from a learning or training perspective. In the case of Anders Ericsson and his colleagues, for instance, the focus has been on the growth of intellectual 'expertise' rather than intelligence as such. Their approach examines questions about the causes of mental competence that have much in common with those problems that are raised by intelligence theorists, while sidestepping the difficulties that have stemmed from the failure to provide a precise definition of intelligence.

Unlike these approaches, the ones I introduce in this chapter stop short of abandoning the basic outlook of intelligence theory, although they criticize and challenge it. Their aim is to create better theories of intelligence. The newer approaches differ from one another in a number of ways, not least in the aspects of the traditional approach that they seek to supersede or replace. Some concentrate on intelligence as a product, attempting to find better ways of describing the forms taken by human intelligence. Others give more attention to explanation, and try to provide better ways of explaining what makes people intelligent and why some individuals are more intelligent than others.

Howard Gardner: The Theory of Multiple Intelligences

Throughout the twentieth century some psychologists have argued for greater acknowledgement of the fact that people can be intelligent in different ways. J.P. Guilford, for example, suggested that general intelligence should be seen as the product of 120 specific abilities. The most influential recent contribution that places stress on the view that there are different kinds of intelligence is that of Howard Gardner, whose book *Frames of Mind* (1984) is subtitled *The Theory of Multiple Intelligences*.

Gardner's approach stems from an awareness that it is common for individuals to be more competent in one field of ability than in other domains, and that many individuals display intellectual strengths that are not reflected in high intelligence test scores. He considers that a theory of intelligence should break away from regarding human intelligence in terms of a single dimension. Gardner feels that there is persuasive evidence for the existence of a number of relatively independent intellectual competences, and he calls these 'human intelligences'. He believes that there are different kinds of intelligence within the same person, and that each of these is to some extent separate and autonomous.

How does one decide what counts as an intelligence, or how many different intelligences there are? Gardner asserts that a case can be made for a separate intelligence existing provided that, first, an area of capability can be identified which becomes highly developed in particular individuals and, secondly, it is possible to identify underlying core abilities. More specifically, Gardner lists eight signs or criteria that function as prerequisites for certifying the existence of an intelligence. He suggests that if a capability exhibits all eight of the signs, it can definitely be classified as forming an intelligence. An ability that exhibited none of them would be excluded, but a capability would not be ruled out as a possible candidate for being a separate intelligence just because it failed to qualify on each and all of the eight criteria.

The eight signs or criteria of intelligence, against which it can be decided whether or not particular capabilities can be regarded as forming intelligences, are as follows:

1 *Potential isolation by brain damage.* The degree to which abilities are genuinely separate or autonomous is indicated, Gardner claims, by the extent to which they can be selectively either destroyed or spared as a result of brain damage.

2 *Evidence from exceptional individuals, such as mentally retarded savants and child prodigies.* These individuals demonstrate that it is possible for a person to have exceptional or precocious abilities in one particular field, whilst the same person's level of performance in other domains is no better than average.

3 *An identifiable core operation or set of operations.* Gardner asserts that an intelligence must possess one or more basic information processing mechanisms that are capable of dealing with specific kinds of input. For example, sensitivity to pitch relationships is a core component of musical experience, with someone whose capacity in this area having an

advantage over others, so far as gaining musical abilities is concerned.

4 *A distinctive developmental history.* For Gardner, an intelligence should have an identifiable developmental history, and it should be possible to identify different levels of expertise through which every novice needs to pass prior to reaching high levels of competence.

5 *An evolutionary history and evolutionary plausibility.* Gardner claims that the roots of contemporary people's intelligences go back millions of years, and that the case for an area of ability that is seen as a possible candidate as a specific intelligence is stronger when it is possible to locate evolutionary antecedents.

6 *Support from experimental psychological tasks.* Examples of tasks that provide this kind of evidence would be ones that cast light on the extent to which abilities are autonomous or otherwise by demonstrating which particular abilities do or do not interfere with one another, or transfer from one context to another.

7 *Support from psychometric findings.* For Gardner, whilst standard psychometric tests play a smaller role in his approach than in the traditional approach to intelligence, they can nevertheless provide further clues concerning the degree to which different abilities are separate and independent of one another. However, Gardner is at pains to point out that high correlations between a person's scores in different areas of ability do not always mean that the abilities are not independent.

8 *Susceptibility to encoding in a symbol system.* This final sign takes the form of evidence that the computations underlying an ability can be embodied in a cultural symbolic system. That criterion is a necessary one partly because in order for a culture to make broad use of a computational system of the brain, the outcomes must be communicable.

Judging abilities that might conceivably be regarded as forming intelligences against the eight defining criteria, Gardner claims that the following separate intelligences can be identified. However, he does not claim that the list is an exhaustive or final one.

- Linguistic Intelligence.
- Musical Intelligence.
- Logico-Mathematical Intelligence.
- Spatial Intelligence.
- Bodily–Kinaesthetic Intelligence.
- The Personal Intelligences.

Ascertaining the extent to which these candidate intelligences actually meet the eight criteria is not always straightforward, but one example, Linguistic Intelligence, will serve to illustrate some of the reasoning involved. Gardner demonstrates that the development of linguistic skills goes through definite and somewhat fixed sequences, and considers evidence for the presence of specific brain mechanisms that facilitate language acquisition. He points out that people who are normal in most respects may exhibit selective difficulties in acquiring language, and he also draws attention to the fact that certain children may be mentally handicapped but with their linguistic abilities selectively spared. Gardner also mentions the existence of 'hyperlexic' children who are mentally retarded and yet at an early age exhibit an ability to read, but with little understanding of the meaning of what they are reading. In addition, he points to research findings pointing to relationships between brain damage and reading disorders.

The above example demonstrates that to a much greater extent than has been usual within the intelligence theory tradition, Gardner has been prepared to look for psychological evidence to provide support for his position. Even so, it is not difficult to find faults with his approach. One is that some of the criteria are somewhat vague, and consequently it is often hard to decide whether or not an ability that might be admissible to the list of intelligences actually meets them. Another problem is that certain narrower and even more specific capabilities than the ones listed above may meet the criteria equally well, and consequently it might be possible to have an equally convincing list of 20 or 30 separate intelligences.

Even with Gardner's criteria, there seem to be no unambiguously correct answers to questions about where to draw lines between different intelligences. All in all, there are no entirely convincing reasons for referring to some abilities but not others as 'intelligences' rather than simply abilities; there is no very clear dividing line between capabilities that are no more than separate abilities and ones that constitute distinct intelligences. Another limitation of Gardner's largely descriptive contribution is that it does not even attempt a fundamental question that traditional theory does at least try to answer, namely concerning why some people are more intelligent than others.

Distinct Intelligences or Separate Abilities? The Talent Account

Considerable uncertainty remains concerning the question of whether or not Gardner's different intelligences are genuinely autonomous and independent, rather than simply being different facets of human ability. The possibility that they really are independent is certainly consistent with the commonsense notion that some people possess innate gifts and talents that are specific to a particular area of expertise. One person, for instance, is thought to be an innately talented pianist, whilst another individual seems to have a gift for painting and drawing. Even within the same family, one child may make fast and apparently effortless progress at learning a musical instrument while an older sibling struggles without much success. Evidence showing that there exists a scientific basis for the belief that specific gifts and talents contribute to human achievements would provide firm support for Gardner's theory, by showing that, at least in some individuals, there is an innate component to the intelligences he designates. The fact that people do differ hugely in the extent to which they make progress in particular areas of achievement seems to provide support for the talent account, according to which innate gifts and talents make an important contribution to individual's achievements.

However, the talent account has been challenged on a number of counts (see, for example, Howe et al., forthcoming; Sloboda et al., 1994, 1996). First, whilst it is true that people differ in their progress towards gaining various skills and abilities, there are usually a number of possible explanations that do not necessitate assuming that the causes must lie in innate differences between people. The varying early experiences of individuals can account satisfactorily for many individual differences in abilities and preferences. Secondly, at least some of the supposed evidence justifying a belief in innate talent is more apparent than real. Investigations have established, for example, that, contrary to what many people believe, high achievers in the arts and sciences are not often characterized by the spontaneous remarkable flowering of abilities in early childhood that is supposed to be indicative of innate talents (Howe et al., 1995). Those children who make the unusual early progress that leads to them being regarded as prodigies have almost always received very considerable help and encouragement prior to the time at which their ability has been seen to be remarkable. Thirdly, research findings challenge the widespread belief that young people differ in their rate of progress in an area of competence to an extent beyond that which would be expected as a consequence of differences between them in their past experiences. For instance, whilst it is true that some young musicians do move ahead much faster than others, the causes probably lie in differences in previous learning, preferences, self-confidence and other qualities arising from individuals' differing life histories. Contrary to many people's expectations, in one investigation of practising in young instrumentalists it was found that the number of hours that very able young musicians spent practising in order to progress from one musical grade to another was no less than the time that needed to be devoted to practising by less able older musicians in order to make the equivalent amount of progress. Even the most creative people need long periods of preparation. For instance, it has been found that all major composers have needed at least 10 years of intensive training to reach the highest degrees of mastery (Hayes, 1981).

Although it is true that people vary greatly in their patterns of abilities, it is quite possible that all the differences between individuals that have been attributed to the existence of innate gifts and talents can be accounted for in other ways, reflecting people's vastly differing lives and experiences. If, as now seems likely, innate talents turn out to be fictions, an implication is that the apparent support they give for the view that Gardner's different intelligences are genuinely independent will melt away, raising the possibility that the so-called distinct intelligences are really no more than different acquired abilities.

Conclusion

Despite the problems I have identified, compared with traditional intelligence theory Gardner's approach does have the advantage of being to some extent constrained by scientific data and based upon hard evidence. At various points Gardner relies on findings from developmental research, knowledge about evolutionary processes, and, particularly, on knowledge of the structure and functioning on the human brain. He is especially attentive to developmental processes, and aware that the form and nature of children's intelligence is constantly changing. In these respects there is a sharp contrast with the beliefs associated with intelligence theory, whose advocates have shown remarkably little interest in the possibility of establishing whether there is any correspondence between their views and what has actually been verified by scientific research concerning the manner in which brains operate, capacities develop, and human abilities are acquired.

Robert Sternberg: A Triarchic Approach

Robert Sternberg, a prolific writer on intelligence, has been at pains to demonstrate that the various phenomena that provide manifestations of human intelligence are more numerous and more complex in their form than is apparent in approaches based on psychometric testing and intelligence theory. For Sternberg the causes, too, are more complicated. Intelligence for Sternberg is nearer to being a broad area of inquiry than to being the relatively narrow topic it represents for traditionalists like the writers of *The Bell Curve* and other recent books within the intelligence theory approach. Unlike them, and in common with Gardner, Sternberg is closely in tune with current research in cognitive psychology; his ideas draw heavily on the findings of empirical research in psychology and the neurosciences (Sternberg, 1985). He is also aware that intelligence is multidimensional, and that intelligent behaviour involves processes and components operating at various different levels.

Sternberg describes his theory as 'triarchic', because it tries to explain the relationships between three different facets of intelligent behaviour. These are: (1) intelligence and the individual's mental world, which refers to the mental mechanisms underlying intelligent behaviour; (2) intelligence and an individual's experience; and (3) intelligence and the person's external world, and how people utilize intelligence in coping with their everyday environments. Here it is clear that intelligence, for Sternberg, is linked both to the outside world of the person's environment and to the internal mechanisms that make intelligent behaviour possible.

In relation to the first facet, intelligence and the person's inner world, Sternberg addresses a number of issues. He is concerned to identify the various components that, together, make a person capable of intelligent behaviour, and to discover how these components actually operate together. For example, he wishes, first, to identify the metacomponents of intelligence. These are the higher order processes that undertake the planning, organizing, monitoring, and evaluation of intelligent behaviour, and select the particular strategies that an individual uses in order to solve problems. Secondly, he also considers lower order processes that are responsible for the detailed spadework that the metacomponents direct and control. There are a large number of these lower order components, each of which is assumed to be relatively specific to narrow ranges of tasks. In addition, and thirdly, there are components that specialize in enabling a person to learn how to undertake the various mental tasks that are made possible by the metacomponents in conjunction with the lower order components they control.

In relation to the second facet of intelligence, Sternberg's theory looks at the ways in which intelligence affects and is influenced by an individual's experiences. He draws attention to ways in which people depend on organized bodies of previously acquired knowledge, or 'scripts', for guiding them through situations that have familiar elements. He also discusses the ways in which people deal effectively with novelty and the manner in which some kinds of information can become automatized.

In his examination of the third facet of intelligence according to his theory, intelligence and the external world, Sternberg is concerned with the outside goals to which intelligent thinking is applied. He sees these as falling into three categories: adapting to environments, shaping environments, and selecting environments. How these goals are achieved greatly depends upon the kind of environment involved. Thus adapting to a family, a job, or a subculture may make very different demands. Being able to shape the environment may be helpful when adaptation is not possible, as when a person adjusts a problem so as to make it soluble by the mental activities at which a person excels. In science, as Sternberg notes, creative individuals often perform a shaping function, setting new paradigms rather than following or adapting to existing ones, and intellectual leaders often create for themselves new styles and new modes of expression. The strategy of selection can be applied on some occasions in which neither adapting nor shaping is possible. For example, the decision to leave a job may be a wise one in circumstances in which a person is unable to adjust to the demands of the working environment and is also unsuccessful at changing the nature of the job so as to provide a better match with the individual's capacities.

Sternberg has produced numerous insights into the different ways in which people think and act intelligently. He has also examined the various mental skills that intelligent behaviours draw upon. Sternberg supplements Gardner's ideas about different kinds of intelligence with suggestions about different ways of being intelligent. For example, he perceives individuals as having different styles of mental self-government. In some people, who are characterized by Sternberg as depending upon a *legislative* style of intelligence, their intelligent behaviours place stress on creating and planning. Others, who place more emphasis on implementing activities rather than planning or inventing them, are regarded by Sternberg as having a primarily *executive* intellectual style. In yet other individuals, monitoring and evaluating are given more importance. These kinds of intelligent activities are typical of someone whose style is primarily *judicial*. Sternberg points out whilst all three of these kinds of activities may be seen in one person, individuals differ in the extent to which each of them predominates.

Stephen Ceci: A Bio-ecological Approach

Stephen Ceci's approach to intelligence is infused with an awareness that, as Vygotsky and his successors such as Urie

Bronfenbrenner have demonstrated, the manner in which individual minds become furnished depends to a very considerable extent on their particular lifetime experiences (Ceci, 1990). These are to some extent unique to each person and are strongly affected in numerous ways by the cultural and family background in which a young person is brought up.

In common with Sternberg, Ceci regards knowledge and mental skills as being interdependent. It is easy to underestimate the extent to which sheer knowledge can affect intelligent behaviour. Ceci has drawn attention to a number of situations in which knowledge differences can lead to people doing better or worse at problems that appear to depend upon kinds of intelligence that go well beyond knowledge as such (see, for example, Ceci and Howe, 1978; Chi and Ceci, 1987). As Susan Carey (1985) has demonstrated, additions to a child's knowledge of biology can produce changes in understanding that ostensibly indicate fundamental changes in the quality of the child's reasoning processes. This finding raises the possibility that the apparently superior thinking and reasoning displayed by people in advanced societies compared with 'primitive' men and women, which seems to point to fundamental differences between people in underlying intelligence, may in reality be largely a product of differences between societies in the cultural knowledge they instil in a growing child.

Ceci shows that the assumption that people can be regarded as possessing fixed abilities, let alone a fixed general intelligence, is highly questionable. In a number of experimental demonstrations (some of which were described earlier, in Chapter 5) he has established that a person's performance level at a task or problem requiring intelligent behaviour may be very strongly affected by the particular context in which the task is presented. Consequently, a person's ability to solve different tasks that are formally identical may vary hugely. The fact that intelligence tests fail to take account of this, and present tasks in context-free circumstances, may result in a person's level of performance at an intelligence test seriously underestimating his or her actual intellectual capabilities. Generally speaking, people who have experienced large amounts of formal schooling will be at an advantage when taking an intelligence test, not because they are genuinely intellectually superior but because they are more accustomed than others to the kinds of context-free or 'disembodied' problems encountered in intelligence tests.

Ceci also places stress on the malleability of intelligence. He cites numerous findings demonstrating that (as we discovered in Chapter 3) under certain conditions IQ levels can either rise or fall very considerably. He is critical of the way in which the general factor *g* has been interpreted. He points out that the fact that *g* emerges as a statistical concept could arise from a conglomeration of reasons, and convincingly argues that *g* has never been shown to have psychological reality as an underlying quality that contributes to individual differences in intelligence.

Mike Anderson: A Cognitive Theory of Intelligence

Unlike Gardner, Sternberg, and Ceci, Anderson is not in principle opposed to the faculty approach of Spearman and his successors. He believes that general intelligence is real, with *g* corresponding to a genuine attribute of thinking. However, Anderson is aware that the traditional intelligence theory approach is not compatible with recent developments in cognitive and developmental psychology, and in neuropsychology. His preferred solution is to look for ways to revise intelligence theory and bring it into line with modern scientific knowledge (Anderson, 1992).

For example, it is now apparent that human cognitive systems are to a considerable extent modular or encapsulated, although the modules do not correspond to the faculties familiar to nineteenth-century psychologists. Modularity involves different cognitive tasks being performed by distinct computational systems, each of which are largely independent of one another and unaware of the others' activities. Thus, for example, the cognitive systems that are necessary for perceiving the visual world operate largely in isolation from the processes underlying language production and comprehension. The brain's modularity is largely innate, but it is also possible for acquired cognitive structures to exhibit some aspects of modularity, particularly when the automatization of mental operations is involved. To take account of the fact that human cognition involves the operation of modular structures, rather than emerging from some kind of unitary general processing system, Anderson's theory incorporates a number of elements that operate in a modular fashion.

Secondly, Anderson is aware that despite the fact that the contents of intelligence tests administered to young children are very different from those of adult tests, intelligence theory has largely ignored the fact that human intelligence develops rather than being static. Anderson's approach is intended to remedy this situation. However, since he wishes to retain some aspects of the *g* concept, which is essentially unchangeable by definition, in order to make allowance for the fact that intelligence does nevertheless develop he is forced to include in his model both developing and unchanging elements.

The outcome is ingenious but cumbersome. A key problem, in my view, is that no attempt to develop a theory which builds on the approach originating with Spearman and improves and elaborates it in order to bring it into line with recent changes in knowledge can be entirely successful. Anderson might have been wiser to build a new approach from scratch, unhindered by the preconceptions and faulty assumptions of what has remained essentially a faulty theory of intelligence. In terms of Sternberg's categories of intellectual functioning, Anderson could have been advised to engage in less adapting to the environment and more shaping of it.

Conclusion

In their different ways, all of these newer approaches emphasize the need for more realism in thinking about intelligence. They all make it clear that there are widely varying kinds of intelligence and differing ways and styles of intelligent thinking. They acknowledge that human intelligence is far from being fixed, and that it is subject to developmental processes. They accept that the idea of intelligence as a kind of faculty of the mind does not square with modern scientific knowledge, and they suggest that intelligent behaviour has numerous different facets and has to depend on many different components and underlying skills. They make an effort to come to grips with the sheer complexity of intelligence, and view the causes of intelligent thought and behaviour as taking the form of complex interacting systems.

Yet despite the fact that all of these newer approaches incorporate attempts to overcome some of the limitations that affect the traditional intelligence theory approach favoured by psychometrists in the tradition begun by Charles Spearman, only to a limited extent have those who remain within that tradition allowed their views to be modified in response to the newer ideas. Much that is still being written about human intelligence, including the work of leading researchers such as Arthur Jensen and Hans Eysenck as well as the most widely read books on intelligence that have appeared in the 1990s, such as *The Bell Curve*, contain little that would seem either unfamiliar or unacceptable to Spearman and his immediate successors at the beginning of the twentieth century.

Why does the older approach seem to prevail? Why, for instance, has *The Bell Curve* made a vastly larger impact than any of the books of Howard Gardner and the other authors featured in the present chapter, despite the fact that its theoretical position is an only slightly modified form of an outmoded and demonstrably inadequate approach that originated at the beginning of the twentieth century?

There are a number of answers. One is that whilst the idea that a person is intelligent to the extent to which he or she possesses some underlying quality of intelligence may be quite wrong, it does have the merit of being simple and easy to understand. Also, as was mentioned earlier, it is an approach that many people find comfortable and comforting, because it accords well with widely shared preconceptions. As I suggested in Chapter 1, if intelligence really was a fixed underlying quality, there would be no need to be too concerned with educational deprivation or with other injustices and inequalities; we could simply accept that what happens to people's lives is mapped out for them by forces outside society's control. Agreeing with the traditional approach to intelligence releases one from an obligation to entertain the uncomfortable view that inequalities are created by ourselves, and are neither natural nor inevitable.

9

Raising Children's Intelligence

Intelligence, as we discovered in Chapter 3, is not the unchangeable trait that traditionalists have insisted it is. Altering intelligence is no more difficult than improving other abilities. That is not to deny that raising a person's IQ is a substantial task. Because an intelligence test samples a number of different cognitive capabilities, more knowledge and more skills have to be gained in order to increase a person's IQ score than is necessary to improve narrower abilities to a comparable extent. All the same, big gains can be achieved. The present chapter examines some of the positive influences that help to make this possible.

Nature, Nurture, and Experience

Customarily, psychologists have placed the various influences on intelligence into either of two categories, 'nature' and 'nurture'. 'Nature' includes all those inputs that are broadly biological, while those that stem from a person's environment are said to belong in the 'nurture' category. This manner of classifying the many kinds of events that affect intelligence has been a tidy way of bringing some order to a multitude of interacting factors. It mirrors the widespread interest in questions about the relative importance of those contributions that come from someone's biological structure and those that reach a person from the external environment.

Unfortunately, though, the practice of dividing the many influences on intelligence into those of nature and those of nurture has a major disadvantage, which has been largely unnoticed. It makes it almost impossible to focus attention on one of the most important forces of all, the person's *experience*. A result of this is that experience has tended to be neglected, because it cannot be made to fit into either the nature or the nurture category. It actually belongs in both.

An account of a young person's early progress will be very impoverished if it fails to give prominence to that individual's experiences. It is not the environment as such but the manner in which that is experienced that determines how each person learns and develops. Psychologists have never denied this, but, confronted with the awkward fact that experience cannot be neatly accommodated within the nature-and-nurture classification, they have evaded the problem. It has been conveniently assumed that assessments of a person's experience can be provided by measuring the person's environment. The implication is that environment is, if not the same as experience, a reliable indicator of it.

Yet that is only true to a very limited extent. Two people can be in precisely the same place at exactly the same time, hearing and seeing identical events, and yet experiencing them in fundamentally different ways. To a keen reader a roomful of books may be a stimulating location; to an illiterate person the same room will represent something very different.

The core disadvantage of using measures of the environment as if they were indicators of an individual's actual experiences is that any such assessment is inevitably one that has been made from outside the person concerned, by someone other than the individual who is actually doing the experiencing. Even when detailed measures of many different environmental factors are available, they only give an incomplete picture of someone's actual learning experiences. Experiencing the outside world is not a matter of just passively absorbing the information the environment provides. Many different influences can affect the way in which a particular individual perceives a given combination of environmental inputs. Among them are the person's existing knowledge, attitudes, interests, temperament, prejudices, mood, and expectations. All these aspects of the individual, and others as well, combine to determine how somebody actually experiences the world that person inhabits, and is affected by life's various events and happenings.

Because any individual's experiences are personal and subjective, and to some extent unique to that person, we can never know exactly how someone else is actually experiencing and learning from their opportunities to acquire new knowledge and new skills. That is not to say that other people cannot influence a person's experiences. Of course they can. For example, parents who make sure that their young child is given opportunities to explore a musical instrument, and provide support when the child expresses an interest in playing the instrument, will be doing much to increase the odds on the youngster learning something about music. Generally speaking, the more we know about a child's attitudes, knowledge, interests, temperament, and so on, the better placed we are to help that child to learn. Knowledge of the individual child does tell parents and others something about how he or she will experience the activities that adults make available.

That is one reason why parents who can really get to know their young children as individuals are in some respects better equipped for helping them to learn than even the most expert teachers. When parents talk to their own children, they can refer to things that they know to be important to the child, such as happenings that play a big part in daily life. Parents are able to do this because they know their child. They are attuned to the child's interests, enthusiasms, and fears. As a consequence of having shared much of the child's life and experiences, they know what he or she does and does not already understand, and what interests him or her. In contrast, any teacher who is responsible for a number of young children is bound to be held back by the absence of detailed knowledge about each individual. The technical teaching skills possessed by a teacher cannot fully compensate for this disadvantage.

Yet even the most capable parents never have total control over their children's experiences, as is evident from the findings of some research investigating brothers and sisters that was conducted by Judy Dunn and Robert Plomin (1990). Imagine a situation in which the parents of two small children strive to establish a regime in which their children are treated equitably. Each child receives the same amount of parental attention and support. Each child is exposed to the same kinds of stimulation, and has opportunities to engage in the same activities. And yet, as Dunn and Plomin discovered, the two children will report experiencing their childhoods very differently. One child, because she has been in the position of being the older one, sees herself as having been treated less indulgently than her sibling, and having had more demands made upon her. The experience of the younger child has been very different. She is aware, for instance, that compared with her sister she has had to go to bed earlier and has fewer opportunities to engage in exciting activities like cutting paper with scissors and eating with a knife.

So although the children's parents may have conscientiously tried to treat each child in exactly the same way at the equivalent age, the older child and the younger child have gained contrasting impressions of the manner in which their parents brought them up. Despite their parents' even-handedness, the two children have had different experiences. For Dunn and Plomin, the lesson to be learned from situations of this kind is that even when children are brought up together, large elements of their environments are not shared between them. Children's environments, these authors assert, are largely 'unshared', even when they have been raised in the same family. An alternative way of viewing this situation is as a demonstration that identical environments do not always produce identical experiences.

The inadequacy of measures of the environment as indicators of someone's actual experiences is also stressed by Urie Bronfenbrenner and Stephen Ceci (1994), who make the point that if a person is to be influenced by certain environmental happenings, those events must in some way impinge upon the person and gain his or her attention. These authors stress that whether that happens or not will depend upon various characteristics of the person concerned. In other words, the real influence of environmental events upon someone depends upon how those events are actually experienced by the particular individual concerned.

Higher IQ or Increased Intelligence?

How can we tell if someone's intelligence has increased? A convenient and objective method is to compare the person's present IQ with their score at some time in the past. However, the sheer fact that intelligence tests are so convenient to use can lead to our investing too much importance in them, and it is important to keep in mind the fact that a person's IQ is just one indication of that individual's intelligence. As was noted in

Chapter 1, the assessment of intelligence that is provided by an IQ score is a somewhat restricted one: it reflects an individual's capacity to act in only some of the ways in which a person can be intelligent.

As we have seen, relying on IQ scores too much, and forgetting their limitations, can be a 'horse before the cart' kind of error, rather like stressing a factory's performance at a 'productivity' test rather than concentrating on the factory's actual output. That the kinds of intelligence that lead to success in real life are not always reflected in high IQ scores is evident from evidence collected by James Flynn concerning job success in Chinese immigrants to the United States. As was mentioned in Chapter 6, it was found that among these individuals below-average IQ scores co-existed with indications of above-average practical intelligence, as demonstrated by doing well at demanding jobs in business and the professions.

Other instances of too much reliance being placed on IQ scores are not uncommon. They can be seen, for example, in assessments of educational interventions such as some of the Head Start programmes discussed in Chapter 3. A programme that has proved very effective at increasing children's practical intelligence, as demonstrated by improved school progress or a decrease in reading problems, may be wrongly supposed to have failed simply because the improvement it has produced in the children's IQ scores has been small or temporary. It is necessary to remember that the real aim of encouraging children to learn more or make better progress is not to raise IQ as an end in itself but to help them gain knowledge and skills that extend their mental skills and capabilities. A frequent side-effect of the improvements is to raise individuals' IQs, and if that happens, well and good. But if an intervention that has successfully achieved its aim of adding to a young person's practical intelligence has not produced a corresponding increase in IQ, that is hardly a tragedy, and certainly no reason for asserting that the intervention has failed. Except for the purpose of gaining admission to Mensa, improving someone's intelligence test score is not a valuable achievement in its own right. The higher score is no more than an indicator that improvement in thinking has taken place. And as we have seen, even as indicators IQ scores are considerably less than perfect.

Providing the Everyday Experiences that Make Children Intelligent

The remainder of this chapter looks at some key elements of those early environments that encourage children to develop into intelligent young people. The focus here is on what happens in a child's own home. Of course, home is not the only context in which events occur that help a child to become intelligent, and parents are not the only people who can help a young child. Yet, especially in the early years, the home is a particularly rich and influential learning environment. And there is the particular practical advantage that parents know their own children as individuals.

Most people are aware that young children need to be stimulated and to be given plenty of attention, but not everyone appreciates just how important adult attention is. Parental interest and attention that is targeted in ways that encourage children to use and extend their abilities is particularly crucial. By way of an illustration of this, recall the major investigation by Betty Hart and Todd Risley that was first mentioned in Chapter 3, which revealed that a powerful predictor of a child's progress in acquiring language is the sheer amount and frequency of adults' talk that is directed towards the child.

'Guiding' is a more appropriate term than 'teaching' to describe the parental activities that are most effective for helping a young child to learn. The young child has something in common with an adult who is visiting an unfamiliar city in an alien civilization. Although that experience is an exciting and stimulating one, and it is obvious to the visitor that there is much that is interesting in this new environment, it may be hard for the newcomer to make sense of what is happening. Despite the wealth of new experiences it is difficult to learn from them, because everything is so confusing. The fact that so much is new and unfamiliar makes it hard to see where to begin to understand it all. What is needed is someone who can guide the first attempts at exploration and understanding, a person who can impose some kind of order on the chaos of experiences, perhaps by directing the neophyte's attention to those objects and events that are especially significant and important.

Having a good guide can make an enormous difference here. The guide can help in various ways, and show the confused individual what to look at and what to listen to.

The young child has a similar need for a helpful guide. Parents are especially crucial here, because they can perform many guiding functions. They help to order the child's experiences, and encourage the child to pay attention to those elements of the surrounding environment that are especially interesting, or especially crucial, or which can provide valuable additions to the child's knowledge.

The actual effectiveness of parents as guides for their young children depends upon a number of factors. These include, for instance, conscientiousness in being attentive, and having the imagination to try to see things from the child's point of view. With very young children it is particularly important for a parent to be attuned to the child's mental state and to be sensitive to the ways in which a baby's needs are communicated. Being attuned to the young child's state is partly a matter of noticing when the child is receptive enough to take advantage of a learning experience. Generally speaking, babies only learn when they are reasonably alert and in the right frame of mind. They do not give much attention to events in the outside world when they are tired or irritable, or when they are hungry or anxious. They will not respond well to a parent's attempts to teach them something new if they are afraid or over-excited. The times when efforts to encourage a baby to learn are most likely to be effective are ones when the child is alert but fairly calm, quiet but not too sleepy. The parent who makes an effort to be attuned to a child's mental state will be well placed to succeed at guiding the young child's development, because that parent is able to engage the child's interest at those times when he or she is most likely to be receptive.

Being sensitive to babies and young children also involves awareness of particular personalities, temperaments, and moods. It is especially important for a parent to learn to respond to the signals that communicate a baby's needs. Research by Mary Ainsworth has shown that babies who make especially good progress tend to be ones whose mothers are sensitive and responsive. These mothers take care to interpret the vocalizations, facial expressions, body movements, and

other behaviours by which a young child's needs are communicated, and they are also quick to respond to those communications. By the end of their first year, children whose
mothers are sensitive and responsive tend to cry less than
others and have acquired more mature ways of communicating.
By the age of four, those children whose mothers have been
most sensitive to their needs in the first year tend to have
higher intelligence test scores than other children.

Parental Structuring of Learning Tasks

The term 'scaffolding' has been widely introduced to describe
certain of the guiding activities that parents undertake when
helping a child learn to do new and unfamiliar tasks. Initially,
the adult takes charge and simply encourages the child to make
small contributions, but later the child makes bigger and bigger
inputs and is allowed to take increasing responsibility for the
task as a whole. The adult carefully monitors the child's progress, and the structuring or 'scaffolding' of the task that was
at first the responsibility of the adult alone is increasingly
internalized by the young learner.

Keeping Learning Informal and Pressure-free

Young children learn best in situations that are relaxed and
informal. The kinds of activities that promote learning often
involve play and games, and are not too tightly structured.
Children only give their full attention to events they find
interesting, and even then their attention spans can be very
short. On the whole, learning experiences are likely to be
enjoyed by the child when they start with objects or events that
the child already finds intriguing, and these are likely to be
ones that have some personal meaning or significance.

Any kind of pressure on a young child, or any action on the
parent's part that leads the child to feel that he or she is failing
to meet the parent's expectations, is liable to be counterproductive. If learning opportunities come to be associated in
the child's mind with pressure or anxiety, the child will avoid
them in the future. Even the best-intentioned parent can put a

child off a learning activity by seeming too eager for the child to succeed or by forgetting how quickly a child can become tired or distracted, or get bored with an activity that was engaging his or her full attention just a few seconds ago. So when a baby or young child begins to lose interest in whatever it is that a parent teacher is trying to bring to his or her attention, there is nothing to be gained by pursuing it. The wise parent will desist for the moment and try again later. A keen adult who persists too long at trying to stimulate a child's learning may simply make the child anxious. Parents sometimes have to restrain their own enthusiasm for the child to learn, and remember to be sufficiently responsive to the child's behaviour to notice when the child's willingness to keep attending begins to wane.

One of the reasons why play and game situations are particularly effective for promoting learning is that they involve parent and child each taking turns, with each responding to the other. Attention is more likely to be sustained when the child's role is an active rather than a passive one. Almost any activity that involves adult and child taking turns to be both active and attentive to the other person is likely to help the young learner to gain useful skills, ones that can be called upon in a variety of situations that involve interacting with other people.

Language

One advantage of game or play activities in which parent and child each take turns to attend to and then respond to the other is that they promote the learning of skills that are crucial components of the conversational activities that are central to human language. I⁺ hardly needs saying that gaining language amplifies the mind: it brings about an explosion in a child's mental capabilities. Once language has been mastered, a young person is not only able to communicate with other people and enjoy all the advantages that the ability to do that brings, but is also much better equipped to think and learn. With language comes the capacity to retain vastly more information than was previously possible. That enables a growing child to begin to make plans, to consider options, to imagine, to remember and build upon past experiences. None of these key abilities are possible for a language-less individual.

Because of the impact of language on the child's mental powers, a young person who masters language especially early or unusually well will gain immense advantages as a thinker and learner. So there is much to be gained by encouraging children to acquire good language skills at an early age. There are two important initial questions to be asked here. First, is it actually possible to accelerate the acquisition of a child's first language? Secondly, if it is possible, how can that be achieved?

Some psychologists have assumed that special efforts to promote language acquisition are fruitless. That view is partly based on the observation that human language has some of the characteristics of an unlearned instinct. For instance, language emerges in some form even in those children whose learning experiences are far from ideal, and we humans can acquire language only because our brains, unlike those of other animals, are innately designed in ways that facilitate language learning. Human brains are not just more powerful than those of other species, but are also pre-equipped at birth in ways that enable language to be rapidly learned. So perhaps parental efforts to stimulate language growth are simply unnecessary. Another reason for holding the view that such efforts may be fruitless is that in a few studies it has been found that formal instruction aimed at improving grammatical correctness in young children can actually impede progress rather than facilitating it.

On the other hand, in some ways human language is not at all like an instinct. In particular, there is ample evidence that the way in which it develops in an individual depends upon the person's experiences. In recent years numerous research findings have established that it is possible to accelerate a young child's language development very considerably. It also turns out that doing so requires no special teaching skills: the majority of conscientious parents are quite capable of helping children to acquire key language skills at a younger age than the average.

Research findings indicate that a key factor in parents' effectiveness at encouraging language development is their willingness to talk to the child in ways that gain the child's attention and engage the child in conversation-like activities.

These can start at as young an age as around six months, well before the child can produce any words at all. Although children do not usually talk in the first year, during this period they can be helped to gain many skills that a language user depends upon, such as taking turns, carefully attending to the human voice, discriminating between similar sounds, and beginning to produce some of the sounds which will form eventually part of the child's own spoken language. Before they can become able to talk, babies have to learn that sounds can represent objects, events, and experiences, and that using language involves two individuals each taking turns to communicate and attend to the other person.

Research undertaken by a number of investigators working independently has confirmed that the single best predictor of a child's progress at acquiring language skills is the extent to which she is exposed to adult language that is directed towards her. The particular kinds of encouragement that are especially effective for stimulating language learning depend on the stage of development the child has already reached. Once a child has begun to speak, there are various things a parent can do to stimulate further progress, such as asking questions, talking about the child's own activities, or acknowledging and repeating what the child has just said. It is often helpful for an adult to talk about something that is already engaging the child's interest.

Interventions that Aid Language Acquisition

The above findings appear to provide strong evidence that language is acquired earlier when parents talk to their child frequently and generally make an effort to include the child in their activities. A possible objection to that conclusion is that since most of the evidence is in the form of observed correlations, or relationships, between measures of parents' talk and the rate of their children's language development, it cannot be taken for granted that the parents' activities are the cause of the children's superior progress. It is conceivable that similarities in the language of parents and children stem from other causes, such as the genetic connections between parents and their children.

However, that objection is effectively countered by the findings of a number of studies in which it has been discovered that when parents make certain changes in their behaviour, for instance by increasing the extent to which they talk to a child, the child's progress at language accelerates. In one study, for example, parents participated in a programme in which they were given training and support aimed at helping them to engage in various activities that have been found to stimulate a child's progress at acquiring language (Fowler, 1990). None of these activities were particularly novel or unusual, and most took the form of game and play routines. There were four main ways in which parents were encouraged to make changes. First, they were told to initiate activities based on language more frequently and more regularly than they would normally have done, thereby increasing the child's exposure to language. Secondly, they learned how to make sure that the language activities they introduced were appropriate to the child's stage of development. For example, parents were advised to concentrate on single-word names for actions and objects at first, and gradually progress to more complex expressions. To help them do this, the parents were given a training manual, as well as picture books and lists of words. Thirdly, there was a requirement to keep careful records of the children's progress. Again, the parents were shown how to do this. Fourthly, and finally, parents were advised to begin introducing language games and language activities at a substantially earlier stage in their baby's life than they would have done had they not been participating in the language acceleration programme.

Despite the fact that this down-to-earth programme involved no special methods or techniques of language training, it was enormously successful. Some of the infants were speaking in sentences by the age of a year, although that usually does not happen until around the twentieth month, and by 24 months some had already uttered five-word sentences. On these and various other indications of language progress, including vocabulary size and the use of pronouns and plural forms, the scores of the participating children were well ahead of the average, and also considerably higher than the scores of children who had been selected to form a control group. Moreover, the beneficial effects were long-lasting, with the advantages that were gained being maintained until the time when the children were last tested, at the age of five. In contrast, the one child who was removed from the programme (a decision made by the mother) slipped back substantially, and, incidentally, his IQ score also went down.

These findings show that big improvements can occur when parents are trained to take a more active role in stimulating their children's language development. Some other research results indicate that even small-scale interventions can make a real difference. For instance, in one study the parents of two-year-olds were provided with information about useful activities to engage in at the times when they were reading stories aloud to their children (Whitehurst et al., 1988). The instructions given to parents were designed to help them to give the children plenty of practice in using language to express their thoughts. To encourage this, the parents were advised to get their children to participate more accurately in the reading sessions. Parents were told to pose various questions, such as 'What?' ones (for example, 'There's the little girl. What's happened to her?') or 'Why?' ones (such as 'Why is the little girl running after the doggie?'), aimed at getting their children to express themselves in words. There was also advice about ways to present challenges that gradually increased in difficulty, making progressively greater demands on the use of active language.

Unlike the previous programme, this one lasted just a month and the parents only needed to be given a small amount of training. Even so, it was definitely effective. Compared with children who formed a control group, whose parents spent an equivalent amount of time reading to them, the participants made substantial gains.

These and other studies have demonstrated that accelerating children's language development is a practical possibility, and does not require superhuman efforts or special teaching skills. Of course, it is still possible to argue that deliberately attending to language development is not really essential, since almost all children do learn to talk eventually even when their home backgrounds are far from satisfactory. But there are two good reasons for rejecting this view. First, since language opens so many doors, enabling people not only to communicate with one another but to start acquiring all the reasoning, thinking, problem-solving and remembering capabilities that language makes possible, a good early start at language brings a child numerous advantages. Secondly, even though a child who is given little encouragement will eventually gain a basic competence to use language, that may not be enough for a person to thrive in the modern world. Nowadays, literacy is important and people require a degree of expertise with language that goes beyond having a merely adequate capacity to communicate.

Reading

Reading does not amplify a child's mind to quite the extent that language does, but it opens some important doors. In particular, it gives the young learner a degree of autonomy and independence, making it possible for knowledge to be expanded even at times when there is no adult present to instruct the child or provide information. Reading also gives a child access to the whole culture of literacy, in which things can be achieved that are simply impossible in an illiterate society. That reading makes it possible for humans to have access to vast quantities of stored knowledge is something that we usually take for granted, but a moment's reflection makes it clear that in the absence of that capacity not only would individual lives be restricted but whole cultures would be prevented from expanding and developing.

For one young child the advantages to be gained from learning to read a year or so earlier than usual may be considerable, but for another child the benefits will be smaller. Much depends upon the extent to which a particular child actually exploits the newly gained capability. In most cases, it would be wise for parents not to be too greatly concerned about whether or not a child reads earlier than others. Generally speaking, if a child is keen to learn to read and parents are enthusiastic about helping, the outcome is likely to be favourable. But not every bright pre-school child will be motivated to read independently, and those who are not can be put off reading by pressure to learn from over-enthusiastic parents.

But even when parents decide against making a big effort to help their child to learn to read, there is an enormous amount that they can do to help the child avoid problems that can arise when learning to read does begin. It is not at all surprising that many children experience difficulties with learning to read, because it is a difficult achievement. The neophyte reader has to gain a variety of different skills and items of knowledge, and combine them appropriately. The many things that parents can do to minimize a child's difficulties fall into two categories. First, parents can do much to make sure that a child really wants to read, and is able to see that there are big advantages in being able to do so. Secondly, parents can also ensure that by the time formal reading instruction at school begins, the child is already well equipped with the various pre-skills that are needed if the learning process is to proceed without difficulty. A child who can already identify at least some letters and can discriminate between similar sounds will find it much easier to make progress than a child who lacks these capacities.

The single experience that does most to prepare a child to learn to read is being regularly read to by adults. Reading to children allows them to discover that books are enjoyable and interesting, as well as useful, and in experiencing for themselves the pleasure to be gained from reading most children will become aware that being able to read on one's own is a highly desirable state of affairs.

As well as reading to children, there are other things that parents can do to help make a child aware of the desirability of being able to read, and also help equip the child with knowledge that will make the process of learning to read easier. One of the ways in which parents can act as guides to their children is by regularly drawing letters and words to their attention, and generally promoting awareness of the importance of writing and print in people's lives. Children are more likely to become familiar with the written word and aware of its possibilities when their parents share with them everyday experiences such as using a recipe or a timetable, consulting written instructions, or finding needed information in a newspaper. Attempts to teach a young child basic pre-reading skills, such as letter identification, are likely to engage the child's interest if they take place within the context of such meaningful daily activities.

Preparing a Child for School Learning

By providing suitable opportunities and encouragement aimed at equipping children with mental skills and knowledge, parents contribute directly to making their children into intelligent young people. Parents also influence the development of their children's intelligence in ways that are less direct, but equally important. In particular, they can do much to equip a child to take good advantage of various opportunities that arise, in and out of school, for extending their mental abilities.

In order to prepare a child for making the best of the opportunities for mental growth that are provided at school, an effective parent helps to make a child capable of thriving in environments that are very different from the child's own home. At school, because adults are in short supply, there will be far less of the one-to-one adult–child interactions that are readily available at home.

There are a number of ways in which varying home experiences can leave children differently prepared to seize opportunities to further extend their mental capacities. First, the young child who arrives at school already armed with mental capacities such as the ability to identify letters and some counting skills will be better prepared for school learning than a child who has yet to gain those basic capabilities. Secondly, and less obviously, a child will be particularly well prepared for school if she has gained certain habits that help a child to engage in the kinds of learning activities through which mental skills are extended. For example, a child who has acquired the habit of listening carefully to the human voice will tend to be considerably more successful at school than a young person whose home experiences have not encouraged her to gain that habit. Similarly, a child who becomes accustomed to playing games in which success depends upon being able to sustain careful attention or close concentration will have acquired additional habits that contribute to her preparedness to take advantages of opportunities arising at school. Thirdly, the extent to which a young person actually succeeds in extending her intellectual capacities in the school classroom will depend to a considerable extent upon her motivation to do so.

Here again, parental support can make a positive contribution. Parents provide this in various ways, for example by ensuring that help is available when a child is experiencing the kinds of difficulties that can lead to someone becoming discouraged or fearful of failure, and by making a child aware of the rewards that follow effort and providing good role models. They can give plenty of opportunities for a child to discover the advantages to be gained from taking an approach to life that involves being mentally active, questioning, curious, and willing to work at solving problems, rather than being mentally passive and learning to regard mental challenges with fear or anxiety.

In these and other ways parents can do much to make sure that their children continue to extend their mental powers even when the parents are not physically present. Of course, teachers play a huge role here, but at least whilst typical classroom ratios of teachers to children remain at current levels, the still common view that a schoolchild's mental development can be left entirely to the child's teachers is somewhat misguided.

Conclusion

There is much that parents and other adults can do to increase the likelihood of a child's early life being rich in experiences that will help the child to acquire useful capabilities. An assumption that underlies much of what has been said in this chapter is that making young people more intelligent is largely a matter of increasing their intellectual capacities by extending their mental skills and adding to their knowledge. However, not everyone would agree with this. Especially within the psychometric and intelligence theory traditions, it is widely assumed that differences in intelligence are far from being just differences in mental knowledge and skills, and that attributes of high intelligence have little to do with knowledge and mental skills. For instance, as we saw in Chapter 2, one frequently mentioned characteristic of high intelligence is 'mental speed'. In fact, differences in speed have been regarded as so central to views about the meaning of intelligence that the speed at which tests are correctly performed has regularly been among the factors determining a person's IQ score. Another widely

accepted characteristic of intelligence that appears to be distinct from specific mental skills and knowledge is mental flexibility or dexterity. It is claimed, for instance, that highly
intelligent people differ from less intelligent individuals in their
capacity to adapt to new circumstances by, say, moving quickly
from one mental task to another or by transferring skills or
knowledge acquired in one set of circumstances to a different
situation.

The assertion that speed and flexibility are characteristics of
intelligent behaviour is uncontroversial. However, that does not
mean that these qualities can necessarily be regarded as basic
causes of efficient mental functioning, or ones that make contributions that are distinct from the effects of improved or
extended mental skills. The argument reintroduces issues
raised earlier, especially in Chapters 1 and 2. There the question was raised of whether certain manifestations of high intelligence should be seen as underlying causes (or explanations)
of individual differences between people, or whether they are
simply differences in performance, and not causes of those
differences at all. For instance, are mental speed and mental
flexibility simply products of high intelligence or is there some
truth in the idea that there exist inherent differences between
people in these characteristics and that these differences are a
cause of individual differences in measured intelligence? Arguments could be made for and against both these viewpoints.
Since intelligence measures can be seen as end-products of
lengthy chains of causes and effects, there are ample opportunities for phenomena that feature the causal chain as outcomes
of prior events to serve also as the causes of subsequent events.
To assume that variables such as mental speed and flexibility
have to be exclusively either causal influences or performance
indicators oversimplifies the true state of affairs.

There is plenty of evidence that people become faster and
more flexible in their performance at various tasks as expertise
improves with increasing familiarity and practice. This may
have the added consequence of enabling skills to be performed
with a degree of automatism, thereby releasing some of the
individual's attentional resources to be directed to other aspects
of the task being attempted. But since there is no firm evidence
that flexibility or speed differences occupy an early place in a
causal chain leading to IQ measures, there are good reasons for

regarding differences in speed and flexibility as being indicators of high intelligence rather than causes. It follows from this that efforts to make children more intelligent are likely to be most successful if they concentrate on helping young people to acquire and practise mental skills. Increased speed and flexibility will be useful by-products of such an approach. It may be true that there is more to variability in intelligence levels than differences in mental skills and acquired knowledge, but even if it is, helping a child to extend these will go a long way towards making the young person more intelligent.

10

Twelve Well-Known 'Facts' about Intelligence Which are Not True

In the light of the evidence examined in this book it is clear that a number of widely shared beliefs and assumptions about human intelligence are simply wrong. In particular:

1   Contrary to the assertions of so-called 'experts' on intelligence, it is not true that different racial groups are genetically different in intelligence. Research findings point to an absence of any genetic differences between races that have direct effects upon a person's IQ score. (See Chapter 4.)

2   It is not true that a young person's intelligence cannot be changed. There is abundant evidence that the intelligence levels of children increase substantially when circumstances are favourable. There are no solid reasons for believing that the skills which are assessed in an IQ test are harder to change than other abilities children acquire. (See Chapter 3.)

3   It is not true that men and women with low intelligence levels are incapable of impressive mental achievements. There are numerous instances of people with low IQs succeeding at difficult problems that demand complex thinking. (See Chapter 5.)

4   Genetic influences do not affect people's intelligence directly, except in rare cases involving specific deficits. There is no such thing as a 'gene for intelligence'. Genes affect intelligence indirectly, but in ways that are not inevitable and depend upon other influences being present. (See Chapter 7.)

5   It is wrong to assume that intelligence can be measured in the way that qualities such as weight and height are measured: it cannot. The belief that IQ tests provide measures of inherent mental capacities has led to unrealistic expectations of what mental testing can achieve. (see Chapter 1.)

6   IQ scores are only weak predictors of educational or vocational success in individual people. In many cases other kinds of information yield more accurate estimates about a person's future performance. (See Chapter 6.)

7   Even when IQ scores do predict a person's success at reaching future goals, that is often only because IQ is correlated with other influences that are better predictors, such as education and family background. (See Chapter 6.)

8   An IQ test score is no more than an indication of someone's performance at a range of mental tasks. The implication that there is just one all-important dimension of intelligence is wrong and unhelpful. Other kinds of intelligence can be equally crucial. (See Chapters 1 and 8.)

9   There is no single process or mechanism of the brain that causes people to be more or less intelligent. The belief in a quality of intelligence that provides the driving force making people intelligent is mistaken. An IQ score is merely an indication of a person's mental capabilities: it does not explain them. (See Chapters 2, 5, and 8.)

10   The average intelligence levels of nations do not stay constant. There have been large changes from one generation to another, and big improvements in some minority groups. (See Chapter 3.)

11   At the highest levels of creative achievement, having an exceptionally high IQ makes little or no difference. Other factors, including being strongly committed and highly motivated, are much more important. (See Chapters 6 and 8.)

12   Early experiences and opportunities exert a big influence on intelligence levels. Parents and others can do much to help a child to gain the mental skills associated with high IQ scores. (See Chapter 9.)

References

Alland, A. Jr. (1996) 'Review of *The Bell Curve*', *Current Anthropology*, 37, Supplement, February: S151–2.

Anderson, M. (1992) *Intelligence and Development: A Cognitive Theory.* Oxford: Blackwell.

Baltes, P. and Reinert, G. (1969) 'Cohort effects in cognitive development in children as revealed by cross-sectional sequences', *Developmental Psychology*, 1: 169–77.

Bell, G. (1996) 'Blacks less intelligent says racist lecturer', *Independent on Sunday*, 14 April.

Berry, C. (1981) 'The Nobel scientists and the origins of scientific achievement', *British Journal of Sociology*, 32: 381–91.

Bouchard, T.J. Jr, Lykken, D.T., McGue, M., Segal, N.L. and Tellegen, A. (1990) 'Sources of human psychological differences: The Minnesota study of twins reared apart', *Science*, 250, No. 4778: 223–7.

Brace, C.L. (1996) 'Review of *The Bell Curve*', *Current Anthropology*, 37, Supplement, February: S157–61.

Brand, C. (1996) *The g Factor: General Intelligence and its Implications.* Chichester: Wiley.

Bronfenbrenner, U. and Ceci, S.J. (1994) 'Nature – nurture reconceptualized in developmental perspective', *Psychological Review*, 101: 568–86.

Cahan, S. and Cohen, N. (1989) 'Age versus schooling effects on intelligence development', *Child Development*, 60: 1239–49.

Capron, C. and Duyme, M. (1989) 'Assessment of effects of socioeconomic status on IQ in a full cross-fostering study', *Nature*, 340: 552–4.

Carey, S. (1985) 'Are children fundamentally different kinds of thinkers and learners than adults?' in S.F. Chipman and J.W. Segal (eds), *Thinking and Learning Skills, Vol. 2*. Hillsdale, NJ: Erlbaum.

Ceci, S.J. (1990) *On Intelligence . . . More or Less: A Bio-ecological Treatise on Intellectual Development.* Englewood Cliffs, NJ: Prentice-Hall.

Ceci, S.J. and Howe, M.J.A. (1978) 'Semantic knowledge as a determinant of developmental differences in recall', *Journal of Experimental Child Psychology*, 26: 230–45.

Ceci, S.J. and Liker, J. (1986) 'A day at the races: a study of IQ, expertise, and cognitive complexity', *Journal of Experimental Psychology: General*, 115: 255–66.

Chase, W.G. and Ericsson, K.A. (1981) 'Skilled memory', in J.R. Anderson (ed.), *Cognitive Skills and their Acquisition*. Hillsdale, NJ: Erlbaum.

Chi, M.T.H. and Ceci, S.J. (1987) 'Content knowledge: its role, representation, and restructuring in memory development', *Advances in Child Development*, 20: 91–142.

Clouston, E. (1996) 'Principal speaks of his disquiet while *g* man rants about "eejit" ', *The Guardian*, 25 April.

Dennis, W. (1941) 'Infant development under conditions of restricted practice and minimum social stimulation', *Genetic Psychology Monogaphs*, 23: 143–89.

Dennis, M. and Dennis, M.G. (1951) 'Development under controlled environmental conditions', in W. Dennis (ed.), *Readings in Child Psychology*, New York: Prentice-Hall.

Dunn, J. and Plomin, R. (1990) *Separate Lives: Why Siblings are So Different*. New York: Basic Books.

Elder, G. (1986) 'Military times and turning points in men's lives', *Developmental Psychology*, 22: 233–454.

Estes, W.K. (1970) *Learning Theory and Mental Development*. New York: Academic Press.

Eysenck (1992) 'Fact or Fiction?', *The Psychologist*, 5: 409–11.

Fancher, R.E. (1985) *The Intelligence Men: Makers of the IQ Controversy*. New York: Norton.

Flynn, J.R. (1980) *Race, IQ, and Jensen*. London: Routledge and Kegan Paul.

Flynn, J.R. (1987) 'Massive IQ gains in 14 nations: what IQ tests really measure', *Psychological Bulletin*, 101: 271–91.

Flynn, J.R. (1991) *Asian Americans: Achievement Beyond IQ*. Hillsdale, NJ: Erlbaum.

Fowler, W. (1990) 'Early stimulation and the development of verbal talents', in M.J.A. Howe (ed.), *Encouraging the Development of Exceptional Skills and Talents*. Leicester: British Psychological Society.

Gardner, H. (1984) *Frames of Mind: The Theory of Multiple Intelligences*. London: Heinemann.

Gardner, H. (1995) 'Cracking open the IQ box', in S. Fraser (ed.), *The Bell Curve Wars: Race, Intelligence, and the Future of America*. New York: Basic Books.

Goodman, A.H. (1996) 'A "just-so story" ', *Current Anthropology*, 37, Supplement, February: S161–4.

Gould, S.J. (1984) *The Mismeasure of Man*. New York: Norton.

Guinagh, B.L. (1971) 'Social-class differentiation in cognitive development among black preschool children', *Child Development*, 42: 27–36.

Harnquist, K. (1968) 'Relative change in intelligence from 13 to 18', *Scandinavian Journal of Psychology*, 9: 50–64.

Hart, B. and Risley, T. (1995) *Meaningful Differences in Everyday Parenting and Intellectual Development in Young American Children*. Baltimore: Brookes.

Hayes, J.R. (1981) *The Complete Problem Solver*. Philadelphia: The Franklin Institute Press.

Herrnstein, R.J. and Murray, C. (1994) *The Bell Curve: Intelligence and Class Structure in American Life*. New York: Free Press.

Howe, M.J.A. (1988) 'Intelligence as an explanation', *British Journal of Psychology*, 79: 349–60.

Howe, M.J.A. (1989a) 'Separate skills or general intelligence: the autonomy of human abilities', *British Journal of Educational Psychology*, 59: 351–60.

Howe, M.J.A. (1989b) *Fragments of Genius: The Strange Feats of Idiots Savants*. London: Routledge.

Howe, M.J.A. (1990a) *The Origins of Exceptional Abilities*. Oxford: Blackwell.

Howe, M.J.A. (1990b) 'Does intelligence exist?', *The Psychologist*, 3: 490–3.

Howe, M.J.A., Davidson, J.W., Moore, D.G. and Sloboda, J.A. (1995) 'Are there early childhood signs of musical ability?', *Psychology of Music*, 23: 162–76.

Howe, M.J.A., Davidson, J.W. and Sloboda, J.A. (forthcoming) 'Innate talents: reality or myth?', *Behavioral and Brain Sciences*.

Johnson, C.M., Bradley-Johnson, S., McCarthy, R. and Jamie, M. (1984) 'Token reinforcement during WISC-R administration', *Applied Research on Mental Retardation*, 5: 43–52.

Kamin, L. (1995) 'Lies, damned lies, and statistics', in R. Jacoby and N. Glauberman (eds), *The Bell Curve Debate: History, Documents, Opinions*. New York: Times Books.

Keating, D.P., List, J.A. and Merriman, W.E. (1985) 'Cognitive processing and cognitive ability: a multivariate validity investigation', *Intelligence*, 9: 149–70.

Klemp, G.O. and McClelland, D.C. (1986) 'What characterizes intelligent functioning among senior managers?' in R.J. Sternberg and R.K. Wagner (eds), *Practical Intelligence: Nature and Origins of Competence in the Everyday World*. Cambridge: Cambridge University Press.

Kline, P. (1991) *Intelligence: The Psychometric View*. London: Routledge.

Lane, C.(1995) 'Tainted sources', in R. Jacoby and N. Glauberman (eds), *The Bell Curve Debate: History, Documents, Opinions*. New York: Times Books.

Lave, J. (1977) 'Tailor-made experiments and evaluating the intellectual consequences of apprenticeship training', *The Quarterly Newsletter of the Institute for Comparative Human Development*, 1: 1–3.

Lazar, I. and Darlington, R. (1982) 'Lasting effects of early education: a report from the consortium for longitudinal studies', *Monographs of the Society for Research in Child Development*, 47 (2–3).

Lewontin, R. (1982) *Human Diversity*. New York: Freeman.

Locurto, C. (1990) 'The malleability of IQ as judged from adoption studies', *Intelligence*, 15: 295–312.

Locurto, C. (1991) *Sense and Nonsense about IQ: The Case for Uniqueness*. New York: Praeger.

Loehlin, J.D., Vandenberg, S.G. and Osborne, R.T. (1973) 'Blood-group genes and Negro–white ability differences', *Behavior Genetics*, 3: 263–77.

McClelland, D.C. (1973) 'Testing for competence rather than for "intelligence"', *American Psychologist*, 28: 1–14.

Miller, A (1995) 'Professors of hate', in R. Jacoby and N. Glauberman (eds), *The Bell Curve Debate: History, Documents, Opinions*. New York: Times Books.

Murray, C. (1996) 'Murray's précis', *Current Anthropology*, 37, Supplement, February: S143–51.

Nash, P. (1990) *Intelligence and Realism: A Materialist Critique of IQ*. London: Routledge.

Neisser, U., Boodoo, G., Bouchard, T.J., Boykin, A.W., Brody, N., Ceci, S.J., Halpern, D.F., Loehlin, J.C., Perloff, R., Sternberg, R.J. and Urbina, S. (1996) 'Intelligence: knowns and unknowns', *American Psychologist*, 51: 77–101.

Nisbett, R. (1995) 'Race, IQ, and scientism', in S. Fraser (ed.), *The Bell Curve Wars: Race, Intelligence, and the Future of America*. New York: Basic Books.

Nokes, C. and Bundy, D.A.P. (1994) 'Does helminth infection affect mental processing and educational achievement?', *Parasitiology Today*, 19: (1): 14–18.

Plomin, R. (1986) *Development, Genetics, and Psychology*. Hillsdale, NJ: Erlbaum.

Ramey, C.T., Yeates, K.O. and Short, E.J. (1984) 'The plasticity of intellectual development: insights from preventive intervention', *Child Development*, 55: 1913–25.

Richardson, K. (forthcoming) *Origins of Human Potential*. London: Routledge.

Rosen, J. and Lane, C. (1995) 'The sources of *The Bell Curve*', in S. Fraser (ed.), *The Bell Curve Wars: Race, Intelligence, and the Future of America*. New York: Basic Books.

Rushton, J.P. (1995) *Race, Evolution, and Behavior*. New Brunswick, NJ: Transaction Publishers.

Rutter, M. (1989) 'Pathways from childhood to adult life', *Journal of Child Psychology and Psychiatry*, 30: 23–51.

Rutter, M. and Madge, N. (1976) *Cycles of Disadvantage: A Review of Research*. London: Heinemann.

Sanders, T.A.B. (1992) 'Vitamins and intelligence', *The Psychologist*, 15: 406–8.

Scarr, S. and Weinberg, R.A. (1983) 'The Minnesota adoption studies: genetic differences and malleability', *Child Development*, 54: 260–7.

Scarr, S., Pakstis, S., Katz, H. and Barker, W.B. (1977) 'The absence of a relationship between degree of white ancestry and intellectual skills within the black population', *Human Genetics*, 39: 69–86.

Schiff, M. and Lewontin, R. (1986) *Education and Class: The Irrelevance of IQ Genetic Studies*. Oxford: Clarendon Press.

Schiff, M., Duyme, M., Dumaret, A. and Tompkiewics, S. (1982) 'How much could we boost scholastic achievement and IQ scores? A direct answer from a French adoption study', *Cognition*, 12: 165–96.

Schlaug, G., Jänke, L., Huang, Y. and Steinmetz, H. (1995) '*In vivo* evidence of structural brain asymmetry in musicians', *Science*, 267: 699–701.

Schliemann, A. (1988) 'Understanding the combinatorial system: development, school learning, and everyday experience', *The Quarterly Newsletter of the Institute for Comparative Human Development*, 10: 3–7.

Schmidt, W.H.O. (1966) 'Socio-economic status, schooling, intelligence, and scholastic progress in a community in which education is not yet compulsory', *Paedogica Europa*, 2: 275–86.

Schoenthaler, S.J., Amos, S.P., Eysenck, H.J., Peritz, E. and Yudkin, J. (1991) Controlled trial of vitamin–mineral supplementation: effects on intelligence and performance', *Personality and Individual Differences*,12: 351–62.

Scribner, S. (1984) 'Studying working intelligence', in B. Rogoff and J. Lave (eds), *Everyday Cognition: Its Development in Social Context*. Cambridge, MA: Harvard University Press.

Sedgwick, J. (1995) 'Inside the Pioneer Fund', in R. Jacoby and N. Glauberman (eds), *The Bell Curve Debate: History, Documents, Opinions*. New York: Times Books.

Sereny, G. (1995) *Albert Speer: His Battle with Truth*. London: Macmillan.

Sherman, M. and Key, C.B. (1932) 'The intelligence of isolated mountain children', *Child Development*, 3: 279–90.

Skodak, M. and Skeels, H. (1949) 'A final follow-up study of children in adoptive homes', *Journal of Genetic Psychology*, 75: 85–125.

Sloboda, J.A., Davidson, J.W. and Howe, M.J.A. (1994) 'Is everyone musical?', *The Psychologist*, 7: 349–54.

Sloboda, J.A., Davidson, J.W., Howe, M.J.A. and Moore, D.G. (1996) 'The role of practice in the development of performing musicians', *British Journal of Psychology*, 87: 399–412.

Snow, R.E. and Yalow, E. (1982) 'Education and intelligence', in R.J. Sternberg (ed.), *Handbook of Human Intelligence*. New York: Cambridge University Press.

Sorokin, P. (1956) *Facts and Foibles in Modern Sociology*. Chicago: H. Regnery.

Spitz, H.H. (1992) 'Does the Carolina Abecedarian early intervention project prevent sociocultural mental retardation?', *Intelligence*, 16: 225–37.

Spitz, R.A. (1945) 'Hospitalism: an enquiry into the genesis of psychiatric conditions of early childhood, 1', *Psychoanalytic Study of the Child*, 1: 53–74.

Stein, Z., Susser, M., Saenger, G. and Marolla, F. (1975) *Famine and Human Development: The Dutch Hunger Winter of 1944–45*. New York: Oxford University Press.

Stelzl, I., Merz, F., Ehlers, T. and Remer, H. (1995) 'The effect of schooling on the development of fluid and cristallized intelligence: a quasi-experimental study', *Intelligence*, 21: 279–96.

Sternberg, R.J. (1985) *Beyond IQ: A Triarchic Theory of Human Intelligence*. New York: Cambridge University Press.

Sternberg, R.J. and Williams, W. (forthcoming) 'Does the Graduate Record Examination predict meaningful succession psychology graduate school?', *American Psychologist*.

Terman, L.M. (1916) *The Measurement of Intelligence*. Boston: Houghton Mifflin.

Tizard, B., Cooperman, A. and Tizard, J. (1972) 'Environmental effects on language development: a study of young children in long-stay residential nurseries', *Child Development*, 43: 342–3.

Tyler, L. (1965) *The Psychology of Human Differences*. New York: Appleton-Century-Crofts.

Wasik, B.H., Ramey, C.T., Bryant, D. M. and Sparling, J.J. (1990) 'A longitudinal study of two early intervention strategies: Project CARE', *Child Development*, 61: 1682–96.

Whitehurst, G.J., Falco, F.L., Lonigan, C.J., Fischel, J.E., DeBaryshe, B.D. and Valdez-Menchaca, M.C. (1988) 'Accelerating language development through picture book reading', *Developmental Psychology*, 24: 552–9.

Witty, P.A. and Jenkins, M.D. (1934) 'The educational achievement of a group of gifted Negro children', *Journal of Educational Psychology*, 25: 586–93.

Zigler, E. and Muenchow, S. (1992) *Head Start: The Inside Story of America's Most Successful Educational Experiment*. New York: Basic Books.

Zigler, E. and Seitz, V. (1982) 'Social policy and intelligence', in R.J. Sternberg (ed.), *Handbook of Human Intelligence*. New York: Cambridge University Press.

Index